The Poetry of Gabriel Celaya
A Thematic Study

𝕾cripta humanistica

Directed by
BRUNO M. DAMIANI
The Catholic University of America

ADVISORY BOARD

The Poetry of Gabriel Celaya
A Thematic Study

Zelda Irene Brooks

Scripta humanistica

20

/ Brooks, Zelda Irene.
    The poetry of Gabriel Celaya.

   √ (Scripta humanistica; 20)
    Translation of: La poesía de Gabriel Celaya.
    Bibliography: p.
    1.Celaya, Gabriel, 1911-   —Criticism and
interpretation. I. Title. II. Series.
PQ6623.U34Z5913   1986   861'.64   86-6417
ISBN 0-916379-27-2

Publisher and Distributor:
SCRIPTA HUMANISTICA
1383 Kersey Lane
Potomac, Maryland 20854 U.S.A.

This Book is dedicated to:
Carol Suzanne
Beloved Sister & Cherished Friend

Contents

PHOTOGRAPHY by Dan D. Carbone

MUSES OF VICTOR HUGO

Introduction

Rafael Gabriel Juan Múgica Celaya Leceta was born on March 18, 1911, in a small Basque town near San Sebastián, the capital of the province of Guipúzcoa. His ancestors on his father's side were Basque industrialists who contributed greatly to their country. When he was very young his family moved to San Sebastián where he completed high school. At 16 years of age he went to Madrid where he received his degree in industrial engineering although from early childhood he had a strong inclination toward writing and literature. He was fortunate in that while attending the University he lived in the *Residencia de Estudiantes de la calle del Pinar* where such men as García Lorca, José Moreno Villa, Salvador Dalí and Luis Buñuel had lived. The influence of the people with whom he associated in the *Residencia* during those years was more important in shaping his life than his career in engineering.[1]

Although Celaya was an outstanding student at the university, he completed his work without any real conviction because of his preference for literature. Upon completion of his degree in 1935 he began work in his parents' industrial concern in San Sebastián. The same year he published his first volume of verse entitled *Soledad Cerrada* (1935) under his real name Rafael Múgica. A few months later he received the award *Centenario Béquer* which

---

[1] In the summer of 1966 I traveled to Spain where I was fortunate enough to meet Gabriel Celaya. Besides our talks at that time on his life and poetry, he mailed me a tape with his biography and a brief discussion of some of his poetry. The information included in this study on his life is taken from these sources; much of the information on his poetry is also greatly influenced by our talks.

1

caused him to strongly consider abandoning his engineering endeavors, moving to Madrid and dedicating his time completely to literature. Unfortunately, in June, 1936 the civil war broke out in Spain, which put an end to such plans.

When the war was over he began work again at his father's business. At this point he was almost completely disillusioned with poetry because it was so different from that he had known as a student at the University; he felt lost. All the poets he had known and admired were either dead (Lorca) or imprisoned (Miguel Hernández) or exiled (Juan Ramón Jiménez, Manuel Machado, Jorge Guillén, Rafael Alberti). Celaya's reaction to this situation was to cease publishing although he continued to write. He did not publish a single line during the ten year period from 1936 to 1946.

However, 1946 was a year of abrupt change in Celaya's life. In this year he underwent a severe psychological as well as physical crisis. The crisis was so severe that he was bedfast for a period of six months. Fortunately, it was also this same year that he met Amparo Gastón, his present wife, whose love and encouragement aided him in overcoming this difficult period. She persuaded him to begin publishing again; together they founded a literary magazine entitled *Poesía Norte* in which Celaya began to publish both his old and new verse. He felt such a complete change had occurred in his poetry and life that he published his new poetry under a new name Juan de Leceta. The two most important volumes he published in this period were *Tranquilamente hablando* (1945-46) and *Las cosas como son* (1946).

This period in Celaya's life coincided with a very significant change in Spanish poetry. In various parts of the country almost simultaneously many poets began to publish a very distinct type of poetry from that in vogue at the time. Blas de Otero began to write in Bilbao, Luis de Crémer and Eugenio de Nora in León, and Angela Figuera y Medich in Madrid. This new poetry was termed *Poesía social*; it contrasted totally with the *garcilacista* or neo-classic poetry which was fashionable at the height of the Fascist regime. The themes of imperial Spain and the flowery Renaissance forms were completely abandoned and replaced with realistic poetry whose themes were centered around what was happening in Spain at the time. Life was portrayed in a simple direct manner with an almost prose-like structure and presented from a dramatic rather than lyric point of view. The new poetry attempted to give voice to what was silenced by heavy government censure. From a political point of view it was a poetry of non-conformity and revolt, admittedly anti-Franquista. Although much of the poetry of this period was undeniably political, Celaya defines it as primarily existential. He feels it was existential due to

2

the preoccupation with daily existence. The subject matter was real in the sense of the present moment, what was happening in the street, those things which are every man's concern. The primary aim was to «dar luz a los mudos y expresar lo que todo el mundo callaba.»[2] The notorious Spanish *Yo* was suppressed; rather than speak of themselves they attempted to reveal the world through themselves. Celaya expressed his attitude toward lyric poetry as opposed to his own almost prosaic style in a radio interview. When he was asked if his poetry was really poetry or not, he answered he did not know and he did not care: «no sé si es o no es, y me tiene sin cuidado. Lo que yo quiero es que sea algo que interese.»[3]

Algo que interese is indeed descriptive of Celaya's entire poetic production. His principal concern, unquestionably existential in orientation, is the predicament of modern man, not only in Spain but in the world at large. This concern manifests itself through various themes in Celaya's poetry. An analysis of these themes, the paradox, consciousness, mysticism and the position of the artist in society, will provide the basis for an understanding of the relationship between form and content in the poet's work, and will reveal him as both an artist, philosopher, and social reformer.

---

[2] Quotation is from tape sent by Celaya.
[3] *Ibid.*

EVE

I
The Paradox

The philosophic essence of Celaya's poetry depends on two major conceptual themes which are closely related: the poet's idea of life through death (resurrection or paradox) and constant change (existential becoming) are at the source of his poetic inspiration, his intellectual concern and his use of symbolic and metaphorical technique.

It is Celaya's contention that man in general with his microscopic vision has seen himself as all-important and his world as the center of all worlds. The poet believes that this is an error in perspective from which the absurdity with which the existentialists are so concerned stems. He expresses it poetically:

> ¡Ah! ¡Ah! En el océano transverberador,
> ¿qué quieren decir «aún» «después»
> «a la derecha» o «no es mi culpa»?
> Nada significa nada. Hay una espira
> mágico-mecánica que gira y gira: gira
> tan rápidamente que ya no se sabe
> si sube, o si baja, o si vertiginosamente
> extática, permanece inmóvil y se devora
> a sí misma transiluminándose, desin-
> tegrándose en el absoluto porque sí
> del acto puro, central y sin objeto. [1]

---

[1] Gabriel Celaya, *Penúltimas tentativas* (Madrid: Ediciones Arión, 1960), p. 11.

4

One of the existential principles closely related to the idea of paradox which underlies the major themes of Celaya's poetry is the idea of abdication of the ego to another center, the *self* of Jungian psychology. *Je est un autre* and *On me pense*[2] are two lines from the French poet Rimbaud which introduce some of Celaya's works dealing with this theme. This idea leads directly into the basic purpose of Celaya's poetry which is the communication of his understanding that man uses but a small portion of his potential powers and forces. Man has within him the possibility of a higher state of consciousness possessed in the past by several men of whom Jesus, Mohammed, Buddha, and Socrates are exemplary. Every man is responsible for attempting to live as they did—one can no longer excuse himself by calling them Gods. Here Celaya's attitude coincides with the existentialists. Men are Gods or rather made in the image of God. For Celaya, as well as for many existentialist writers, Jesus and Buddha and martyrs of lesser degrees were not Gods. They were only men, but yet they were sons of God as well. They were *Hombres-Dioses*.[3] This lays a heavy burden of weight— the weight of responsibility on man's shoulders, for he too can be Godlike if he so wills.

Celaya advocates a new religion of enlightenment, or a revivification of the ancient ones, springing primarily from poets and artists—literature, painting and sculpture.[4] He challenges every man, and in particular artists, with the responsibility of the revitalization of the social system. This is the positive chord in Celaya's attitude that distinguishes him from some of the more negative existentialists.

Celaya's philosophy, in spite of its similarities in many senses to religious poetry, and obviously tremendously influenced by the teachings of both Christ and Buddha, is nevertheless unique. His is a somewhat eclectic type of poetry as far as influences are concerned. The definition of existentialism in a *Readers Guide to Literary Terms* illustrates how closely Celaya's attitudes parallel this philosophy:

> Both groups of existentialists Christian and non-Christian hold certain elements in common: the concern with man's being; the feeling that reason is insufficient to understand the mysteries of the universe;

---

[2] Gabriel Celaya, *Poesía* (Madrid: Ediciones Giner, 1962), p. 13.
[3] Gabriel Celaya, *Dos Cantatas* (Madrid: Revista de Occidente, 1964), p. 39.
«No somos quienes fuimos. No seremos
nada hasta que aceptemos el trabajo
que ha de hacernos quien somos: Hombres-dioses.»
[4] Gabriel Celaya, *Poesía Urgente* (Buenos Aires: Editorial Losada, 1960).

the awareness that anguish is a universal phenomenon; and the idea that morality has validity only where there is positive participation.[5]

Celaya's philosophical orientation is quite complex. It is simplified, however, by its constant point of origin which is the idea of the possibility of the evolution of man's consciousness.

The «*Mono*,» a character in the drama poem analyzed in detail in Chapter II, is Celaya's best example of the «*homme existencial*» in that he expresses the antithesis to the positive argument of effort and responsibility proposed by the poet. *Mono* laments the near impossibility of man acquiring these new gifts of enlightenment—the work and sacrifice and suffering involved in achievement. He portrays the traditional feeling of futility at its overwhelmingness, the feeling of anguish in the face of solitude and consistent absurdity within which one is obliged to live, if he does not take the easy way out—suicide—physical or other. To the pleas of *Mono* to be allowed to kill himself, *Ingeniero*, the protagonist, makes his reply as to the level of such pleas and such ideas:

> Tus virtudes, hermano, son burguesas.
> Morir sería fácil. No algo heroico.
> Porque quienes se niegan a sí mismos
> son cobardes sin más, y miserables.
> No llames con mentira, sacrificio
> a esa comodidad de la renuncia.
> No queremos que sufras. No admitimos
> que debas inmolarte. Tus virtudes
> son arcaicas, estúpidas y tristes.
> Ni cuentan en el mundo que yo anuncio,
> ni podrían mover la hoja de un árbol.
> Pedimos la alegría del esfuerzo,
> la risa entre dos golpes de martillo,
> el agua como va, y en las turbinas,
> organiza una fuerza constructiva.
> Así vamos haciendo lo posible.
> Son pequeños esfuerzos lo que cuenta:
> Minutos y minutos padecidos,

---

[5] Karl Bechson and Arthur Ganz, *A Readers Guide to Literary Terms* (New York: Noonday Press, 1960), p. 56.

6

días sordos, difíciles, tenaces,
materias que resisten tercamente
y manos revestidas de herramientas
que de pronto son limas, alicates,
tijeras, o garlopas, o cuchillos,
y el fuego bien domado, y el sistema
que organiza el conjunto, y así salva.
Esto es lo que cuenta, Mono hermano.
No ver que en lo real, la trascendencia
declara ese misterio de que existen
las cosas como son y no la nada.
No quedarse suspenso preguntando
por qué existen los seres y no el cero.
No sólo contemplar, neutral y ausente,
el mundo de los hombres y los dioses.
No lavarse las manos ante ciertos
horrores cotidianos. No negarse
y pedir el descanso de la muerte
cuando hay tanto que hacer, y tanto fango,
sin haber aportado nada al orden.
Tu deber es vivir: Luchar alegre.[6]

Work and effort are the solutions offered by the Ingeniero and Celaya.
But how? In such a seemingly meaningless universe is *Mono*'s question.
Moreover there is love and beauty, and who has time to work if delight can
be had? Unfortunately however delight does not come without pain at its
ending, and all things end and change. Change is one of the key ideas in Celaya's poetical system, as well as existential and Buddhist philosophy.

Mono: «Nada permanece, todo vive.
El momento es lo total.»[7]

Celaya himself terms his early work existential. He says it was intended as a
type of social poetry—an attempt to deal with what was, i.e., the daily experiences of life. This led quickly to a type of existential questioning which

---

[6]   Celaya, *Dos Cantatas*, pp. 51-53.
[7]   Celaya, *Dos Cantatas*, p. 25.

has continued throughout his poetry and become best delineated in his most recent volumes.

Celaya in his relationship to the existential idea of the absurd is more anxious to express the experience of absurdity rather than its philosophy. That is precisely why he chose poetry. Reading Celaya's character sketches one is reminded of the French existentialist Gide and his gratuitous heroes who passed to the other side of despair.

One of the best syntheses of the basic similarities or tenets of the existential point of view is given by Julian Palley:

> It is the recurrence of certain themes that suggests a common ideological basis on the part of these writers: These common motifs or focal points of contact may be summed up as follows:
>
> (1) *Existence precedes essence*, the wish to return to the living, breathing person, the *hombre de carne y hueso* of Unamuno, to the subjective and concrete, away from the objective and abstract of traditional philosophy. The existentialist abandons the attempt to describe the world in abstract terms, which, he believes, is impossible; he tries to describe the *situation* of man in the world; man who makes his own essence, day by day, living it.
>
> (2) *Despair*. Kierkegaard, and after him Unamuno, spoke of the struggle between reason and life which produces despair, a condition necessary for the final «leap» to religious faith. In Sartre and the agnostic, atheistic, existentialistic despair would be the condition for discovering morality (according to Samuel Beckett: «Life begins on the other side of despair.»)
>
> (3) *Nothingness, the nada*. Nothingness exists all around man; in order to perform any action, he must cross it. In Heidegger nothingness is a threatening abyss which causes dread or anguish in man.
>
> (4) *Freedom*. Man is completely free, and he must create his own essence, by crossing nothingness. «Man is condemned to be free, and he carries on his shoulders the weight of the entire world.»
>
> (5) *Choice*. Because man is free, he must *choose* continually.

(6) *Responsibility.* His freedom and the constant exercise of choice make man responsible for himself and all humanity (therefore existentialism is an ethical philosophy).

(7) *Anguish.* On choosing between alternatives, on creating his own future, man feels anguish. He is anguished at the knowledge of his total freedom, and at the threat of nothingness.

(8) *Absurdity.* Man finds himself in an unknown world, without fixed values or faith, a victim of irrational forces. (The idea of the absurd occurs above all in Camus and Kafka.)

(9) *The other.* This idea, developed by Sartre, the «*other*» exists as an object for us. The presence of the *other* disturbs our world, threatens the unity we feel, and threatens to absorb our consciousness or freedom in his, that is, to make us an object. For Sartre, original sin is the existence of the *other*. In fine: we have the vision of man standing on the edge of nothingness which, along with his absolute freedom of choice, produces (in) him anguish. His world, therefore, is absurd; but on this foundation of despair, anguish, and complete candor with himself, there exists the possibility of constructing a new morality, a new ethic or faith. Of course, this is an oversimplification, but it may be useful in discovering a unity in the mass of diverse or contradictory elements known as existentialism.[8]

In each of these definitions one finds the exact duplication of Celaya's ideas—not to say that he stops at this, but he does include it. All of the existential writers include these ideas. However, some put emphasis on one aspect and others on another. The French existentialist Albert Camus' point of emphasis was the absurd: *l'homme absurde;* Celaya's the «other»: «*el otro.*» Celaya introduces his only novel entitled *Lo uno y lo otro* with the quotation from Rimbaud already mentioned: «Car je est un autre.»[9]

Celaya's poetry parallels the existential approach in many respects: the constant emphasis on the concrete rather than abstract; the anti-rhetorical, anti-lyrical, prosaic tone of his verse; and his insistence on saying only that

---

[8] Julián Palley, «Existentialist Trends in Modern Novel,» *Hispania,* No. 44 (1961), pp. 21-26.

[9] Gabriel Celaya, *Lo uno y lo otro* (Madrid: Seix Barral, 1962).

necessary. «Tuércele el cuello a lo innecesario,» he shouts. The main virtue of Meursalt, the famous protagonist of *L'Etranger*, was, in Camus' own words, his refusal to say more than he felt.

Celaya's ideas parallel those of Camus in many aspects, but they are couched in different terms. Camus speaks of two levels of suicide—philosophical and physical. These two terms describe the two methods by which man can escape coming to terms with enlightenment. One must not take these escapes, but rather maintain a constant awareness of the absurd and in full view of it not to suffer—because you choose not to. And God? The answer simply that we do not know, is the existentialist's dry answer. Suicide to Camus means not *dying* but *not living* or *never being born*. Suicide is a paradoxical term, poetically used here, since it implies logically that one has lived before in order to die and any new birth would not be birth but rebirth.

Another important parallel found between Celaya and Camus and the existentialist's literature of revolt is the idea of each man's human responsibility to himself and others. Chapter V of this study is a complete development of this idea. John Cruickshank states that this idea is found in all existential literature:

> One finds a continual insistence on the fact of human responsibility. The picture that emerges is one in which the individual is bereft of all metaphysical aids. There is no supernatural authority to which he can appeal. There are no inherited values on which he can rely. He must fashion his own destiny in complete isolation. The literature of revolt presents life not as an established order but as an order to be established. [10]

Celaya's poetry is a careful study of man from these existential perspectives. It is not simply a set of conclusions drawn after the study but a detailed revealing of the factors involved in arriving at these conclusions. His poetry is a complete development of his ideas on the nature and state of man and his possible psychological evolution: the development of will, the power to do what one wants, to achieve freedom and happiness. The principal theme of Celaya's work is an exploration through poetry of man's present state of consciousness and its social, political, and cultural implications as well as the means and circumstances which must exist to heighten it. The foundation of

---

[10] John Cruickshank, *Albert Camus and the Literature of Revolt* (New York: Harper & Brothers, 1958), p. 10.

Celaya's concept of man and the possible psychological evolution with which he is so concerned is the paradox. The poet's initial picture is the paradoxical nature of life. [11] The term or symbol he uses to express this attitude or idea of paradox is the equation of todo y nada, which is consistent throughout his work. [12] One can hear almost simultaneously men like Calderon proclaiming: «la vida es sueño y los sueños, sueños son,» and Quijote proclaiming: «fe hay que tener fe.» But the latter had faith in only dreams and behaved better than those who had faith in reality, or perhaps his dreams were real; «la Realidad osilante» is indeed a profound question now as it has always been for men with enough courage to look upon its face. Plato's discussion of opposites evolving from one another also throws a great deal of light on the nature of the idea Celaya examines through his poetry. [13]

Celaya's attitude toward life as a paradox is founded on his belief that man is born and remains unconscious or asleep (en sueño), unless he learns through some extraordinary set of accidental circumstances the importance as well as the method of awakening, and is then capable of sufficient effort to use what he has learned. Thus in a certain very real sense man is dead although he is existing, and only by realizing his death can he gain the proper perspective from which to work for life. It is quite similar to religious ideas of rebirth. One must die to live then, or at least admit death to live since death is already a fact. This is a constant theme in almost all mystic poetry and it is precisely here that much of Celaya's poetry parallels that of the mystics.

It is interesting to note that the dictionary itself in defining paradox gives two contradictory explanations—as though to reaffirm its nature:

F. para. beside, beyond, contrary to + doxa—opinion.

Fr. to think, suppose, imagine.

1. A tenet or proposition contrary to received opinion, also an assertion or sentiment seemingly contradictory or opposed to common sense, but that yet may be true in fact.

---

[11]   One is reminded reading his poetry, of the picture used for an advertisement of Morton's Salt which has on the picture a picture of the same thing, which has on it a picture of the same thing, which has on it a picture of the same thing, etc., etc. to infinity one can suppose—only with Celaya it becomes a paradox within a paradox within a paradox.

[12]   si decido morirme, eso exalta mi vida
    este ser, confundido, todo y nada. (Gabriel Celaya, *Poesía* (1934-1936) (Madrid: Ediciones Giner, 1962), p. 227.

[13]   *Dialogues of Plato*, Edited by J.D. Kaplan (New York: Washington Square Press, Inc., 1962), pp. 86-90.

2. A statement actually self-contradictory or false.

3. Any phenomenon or action with seemingly contradictory qualities or phases. [14]

However the most satisfactory definitions of the term paradox are found in *Webster's Dictionary of Synonyms*:

> A paradox is primarily a statement or proposition which contains a contradiction yet which, absurd as it seems to be, may still be true and in accordance with the facts and common sense.
>
> A paradox is a situation which is known to exist, yet which when described or put in words seems incredible because it involves a logical contradiction. [15]

These definitions show the extent to which reality and its meaning have to do with one another. Reality is its meaning, felt not intellectualized. From Celaya's point of view it is a question of unity or rather of gaining unity if it is possible. On the whole he is positive rather than negative as to the possibility of gaining unity. The first step is to understand deeply such things as the mechanical nature of all life, including man. Man is a creature of illusions. He imagines himself even, taken quite simply and literally, rather than philosophically. He imagines he possesses powers he does not and it is only through the realization that it is not fact that opportunity for change will present itself. Thus man must know himself for the machine that he is in order to get it to working properly.

Celaya develops a complete system in his work as to the necessary disciplines, principles and methods for gaining the self knowledge required to bring man to his legitimate state: consciousness. A complete discussion of these ideas is given in Chapter II. At present it is sufficient to establish that the foundation of Celaya's philosophical viewpoint toward life and his basic method in style is the paradox. All of the volumes of the author's poetry as well as prose illustrate this foundation. His is an investigation of the age old question of appearance and reality.

It is important to note that this paradoxical attitude toward life exists on

---

[14] *Webster's New International Dictionary*, 2nd ed. unabridged (Springfield, Mass.: G&K Merriam Company, 1959).

[15] *Webster's Dictionary of Synonyms* (Springfield, Mass.: G&K Merriam Co., 1942).

two principal levels: the mystic or symbolic, and the practical. The necessity of death for life on the symbolic level refers to the possibility of attaining consciousness if one releases (lets die) the old divided, mechanical self. This non-existing of the divided unsure self leaves space for the birth of a united or enlightened self which understands its inter-relatedness with all things. This idea is evident in his earlier verse but becomes more explicit as the poet matures. In «Vida de la materia» written in 1935 the method of expression is much more esoteric and mystic:

¡Oh cuerpo, cuerpo
que para vivir, como un hombre, se está destruyendo!
Sé que la luna te quisiera muerto en blanco,
tendido bajo sus árboles de alcanfor congelado.
y sé que el mar te sueña estatua de salitre
luciente aparición en la blanca inconsciencia,
en la masa flotante, traslúcida y sin alma
de las medusas lunáticas y opacas. [16]

In his later verse he states the problem in a more straight-forward manner:

Sois reyes encantados
sois príncipes antiguos y futuros
una conciencia pulsa
tras vuestros mascarones animales.
¡sois tanto! No sabéis.
sois monstruos sin palabras
no seres sin angustia iluminante
sino dioses dudosos
y yo como vosotros! [17]

On the practical level the necessity of death for life is evident.

Solamente— ¡qué pena!— si vivo voy muriendo. [18]

One simply does not exist without the other. Thus to feel anguish over death

[16] Gabriel Celaya, *Poesía*, p. 36.
[17] Gabriel Celaya, *Dos Cantatas* (Madrid: Revista de Occidente, 1964), p. 19.
[18] Gabriel Celaya, *Poesía*, p. 193.

is foolish; it is simply an unawareness of the necessary nature of things, or an unwillingness to accept them, which ultimately amounts to the same thing. Plato's philosophy of opposites coincides perfectly with Celaya's on this point. Plato takes the idea that all things are generated out of their opposites to its furthest point and concludes that there is life after death. Because life comes out of death as death out of life:

> ...but I am confident that there truly is such a thing as living again, and that the living spring from the dead, and that the souls of the dead are in existence, and that the good souls have a better portion than the evil. [19]

Thus Plato removes the argument to another and even higher level which Celaya also attempts to understand. However the latter's conclusions are not so well formulated. Indeed Celaya's belief in an after-life cannot be discerned in his poetry other than by assumption in view of the strong positive element in his attitude toward life and the strong Buddhist influence on his thinking which stresses reincarnation.

Rather than affirmations of a belief in God or an after-life one sees primarily in Celaya's poetry his fervid desire to believe in the traditional concept of man with a purposeful life. But he can no longer believe this. The age of science and the awakening of man to his own history have too clearly pointed out the improbability of the traditional ideas of the how of things. More and more as Celaya's ideas mature he comes to the understanding that the circumstances of history and the nature of man's unawareness have brought him to the state of affairs in which he finds himself today in the twentieth century. The key to correcting this situation lies in an individual man's capacity to be aware of it—to be awake. Only thus can efforts be made to overcome mechanical habits which cannot lead toward the aim desired. This mechanicalness or sleep and consequent suffering Celaya believes is a cosmic law, that is as it is by necessity. [20] Therefore the possibility of escape is very slight and only attained by few. Ultimately not a perfect solution but the only one nevertheless. When man is no longer caused by external circumstances, then and only then he has control, will, freedom, unity, self—he is. He is then capable of being happy if he chooses. «Porque sí» as Celaya puts it, and not because of external or internal circumstances. He is no longer

---

[19] *Dialogues of Plato*, Edited by J.D. Kaplan, p. 90.
[20] Gabriel Celaya, *Dos Cantatas*, p. 57.

sleeping: «Muerto boca arriba.»[21] He awakes, he understands enough to *be* independently of external circumstances an integrated thing moving through life. He is no longer mechanical.

The idea of consciousness and paradox being related to esoteric doctrines is found consistently in literature and art as well as religion. In Celaya's poetry, indeed, it becomes the primary concern and does not alter through the years except in vehicle of expression.

In one of his earlier poems, entitled «Entrando en el bosque,» which is also representative of his most mystic writings, the idea of life in death is evident. The subtlety of metaphor is extraordinary. The close parallel of a deathlike state and lack of control of consciousness is salient; external forces control man. He must respond to them: «Cuando el Bosque palpita, algo en mí le responde.» They are blind forces that respond below one's thoughts.

> ¡Oh cuerpo, qué nostalgia de carreras veloces
> confundido en tropel con las fuerzas primeras!
> Cuando el bosque palpita, algo en mí le responde.
> Rompen, ciegas, las fuerzas bajo mi pensamiento.[22]

But from this very realization there seems to flow a seeking after a new way—a way of change. He abandons himself suddenly to self-searching life-searching.

> La tierra habla con voz de siglos olvidados:
> ¡Oh calor maternal al entrar en la noche
> que un tam-tam o mi pulso, la obsesión alucina!
> ¡llevadme, bacantes, oh vida potente!
>
> Ya dentro del bosque, me detengo, me espanto:
> Son hojas que se agitan, mi sangre apresurada,
> y en la playa lejana, dos olas que retumban,
> dos olas que golpean la soledad del mundo.[23]

His trip was an inward one rather than external. One is reminded of

[21]   Gabriel Celaya, *Poesía Urgente*, p. 13.
[22]   Gabriel Celaya, *Poesía* (1934-61) (Madrid: Ediciones Giner, 1962), pp. 46-47.
[23]   *Ibid.*, p. 46.

Marcel Proust's inward journey—*la recherche du temps perdu*. This inward seeking is a constant theme or technique in Celaya's poetry.

> Oh noches, cuando absorto, hundiéndome en mí mismo (p. 21).
> Su presencia, mi reflejo, me vuelve hacia mí mismo,
> Me hunde poco a poco en mis céntricos abismos,
> Me lleva hasta esa blanca catedral del silencio,
> Donde la luna es la virgen desnuda que yo adoro (p. 14).
> Así me he ido agotando, volviéndome hacia dentro,
> por ansia de unos ojos cerrados para siempre (p. 26).
> insistente me hunde hacia dentro una muerte
> que pesa justamente lo mismo que mi cuerpo (p. 42).[24]

Then again suddenly at a certain climactic point in self seeking he comes to an understanding of his sleep—his sleep in life—and he wants to change. The dramatic structure of the poem is evident. One finds complication, climax and denouement. However the organization is somewhat unorthodox. First occurs the climax or high point of understanding that took place in self seeking and observing. Second is the realization of man's true insignificant, indeed minute, place in the overall scheme of things, and moreover his helplessness—his sleep: «vida aprisonada.» Third comes the desire for change—the willingness even to admit death in order to live. To accept what is as necessary and therefore just: «Quiero morirme, quiero la vida sin nombre.» Yet he wants to be part of the whole, not one lone hero with consciousness, and struggle and tragedy and sin; the man who sees himself and creates himself. The reason? Value. In reality only the absolute exists, the first mover: *Prima mobile*, the will of God. We are all merely reflections of the ultimate pattern. The following verses show the mystic union of love, or creation, and destruction—amor muerte—vivir muriendo, a paradox permeating life.

> Soy un ansia sin brazos,
> soy un dedo sin mano, soy un grito sin boca,
> soy un cuerpo cerrado
> que la sangre golpea buscando salida.

---

[24]   Gabriel Celaya, *Poesía*.

La atención agiganta, mi latido pequeño.
¡Vida aprisionada! ¡Pulso de la angustia!
¡Quiero labios, amor! Que el dolor me abra heridas.
cauces anchos, y quiero
que mi sangre se vuelque por ellos
con su libre abundancia a la tierra.

Quiero morirme, quiero la vida sin nombre,
no el Héroe destacado del Coro con que empieza
la tragedia, la lucha, la conciencia, el pecado,
el hombre que se mira a sí mismo y se piensa.

Hoy sé que sólo vale el empuje primero:
la raíz que socava con su sangre y su llanto,
la tromba que me arrastra, que me ama y destruye:
¡Tierra! ¡Vida ciega! ¡Muerte grande! ¡Te amo![25]

Other examples of self-seeking or struggle after self-knowledge and self-understanding are found in *Penúltimas Tentativas*, one of his volumes of prose-poetry, which is permeated with existentialism. He discusses again the type of remembering or understanding one possesses, not with the memory of the mind but with an indefinite *hedionez* of the flesh; an impersonal type of remembering that exists unconsciously or at least exists without going through the ego.

Recuerdo: ¡Recuerdo tanto ! Pero no con la memoria, en la luz, sino vaga, entrañable, cenestésicamente, con la indefinida hediondez de la carne y de unas células anónima y brutalmente proliferantes que, latiendo en la ciénaga, puntúan resplandores, dudan, vuelven, insinúan como en sueños un posible sistema, tantean con órganos tiernamente torpes y recientes las tinieblas, llegan hasta tocar el límite pensable, mas, ¡ay!, irritadas, se retraen en seguida con un estremecimiento metafísica y dolorosamente animal.
Nada me autoriza a decir que soy yo quien recuerda así. Uno recuerda. Es decir, algo no personal funciona en Uno como recuerdo, si recuerdo puede llamarse a ese rastro carnal anterior a la conciencia. Mas aún con esto, salvada la cuestión metagramatical del sujeto, ¿qué

---

[25] Gabriel Celaya, *Poesía*, p. 47.

quiere decir, cuando se llega a estos extremos, recordar? ¿Resplande-
cer? ¿Hundirse desapareciendo? ¿Sorprenderse a sí mismo por la es-
palda?

Hablo de una presencia que no es enteramente humana, y en mí
vive aún,y seguirá viviendo baja o altamente después de mi muerte
como vivía antes. No antes de lo que llamo mi nacimiento, sino antes
del tiempo, elemental, amortal, fuera de curso, transmental, como
ahora, ahora mismo, sin yo.[26]

This anguish at being flesh is very personal. He laments that he can go
no farther than the outer edges of the self, because it is the self which limits
one's understanding all or anything objectively. The thought always exists
that perhaps without the self nothing could be known. It is my contention that
poetry or prose attempting to express a mystic state or an experience of
higher consciousness in order to be truly enlightening (and give a real feeling or understanding which approximates the one felt by the poet) must do
with language precisely what Celaya has done. He must seek the slippery
edges of logic where opposites mesh and reality by excess becomes non-
reality. If you go far enough away you will be coming back at the same time.
Again the paradox. All of Celaya's work arrives there by one channel or
another.

---

[26] Gabriel Celaya, *Penúltimas Tentativas* (Madrid: Ediciones Arión, 1960), pp.
10-11. This volume was written several years earlier but not published until 1960.

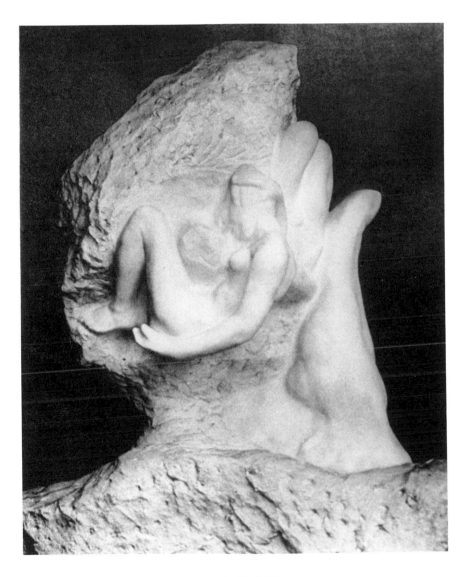

HAND OF GOD

II
Consciousness

Celaya best portrays his principal theme, man's situation in sleep or lack of consciousness, dramatically in a poem entitled «El derecho y el revés.» The language spoken by the characters is prose poetry with a rhythm harmoniously in tune with his theme at every point. The protagonist is Prometheus, an Engineer.[1] He is a conscious man, an exception among the crowd who have not yet evolved. The crowd, the majority of humanity as well as the engineer's sons are called *Zomorros*, a Basque name describing the animal masques used in carnivals in that region of the Pyrenees. Epimetheus, Prometheus' slower thinking brother is *Mono*: monkey. The name itself suggests Darwin's theory of the evolution of man from the primates which is the basis of Celaya's own ideas as to where man is to go next in evolution. *Mono* is not yet conscious, but realizes the possibility exists if he is willing to sacrifice his old habits and ways of life. *Ezbá*, the female in the drama, is symbolic of the paradox of Pandora which represents the philosophic standard placing life on a contradictory scale or equivalent of a yes-no basis.

A closer examination of the details of the myth as well as its modern parallel in Celaya's dramatic poem will illustrate the detail of the philosophy

---

[1]   En el trasfondo de esta cantata late la vieja fábula de Prometeo y Epimeteo. Pero dado la forma que han tomado en mi circunstancia estas imágenes primeras, me ha parecido necesario cambiar los nombres de los protagonistas. Así Prometeo ha pasado a ser Ingeniero; Epimeteo, el mono y Pandora, Ezbá. Ezbá o Ez-bay—el verdadero nombre de Eva, según el pintoresco abate Lahetjuzan—es un patronimico vasco que literalmente traducido significa «no-sí», y me ha parecido por eso adecuado para designar la voz femenina de esta cantata. (Gabriel Celaya, *Dos Cantantas*, p. 13).

of the nature of man and his relationship with the world.

Prometheus is a Greek word which means forethought. It is also the name of one of the Greek gods, the most clever among them, an inventor. It was he who filled the earth with animals and men.

Epimetheus, which means afterthought in Greek, was unfortunately just what his name implies, a man who thinks afterwards when it is too late. In spite of his brother's warning against possible vengeance on Zeus' part, he accepted a wife from Hermes, Zeus' brother. This wife was Pandora, or all gifts, created by Zeus and blessed with a gift from each of the gods. She was the first woman and became the mother of all women.

Pandora, in spite of the gifts of beauty and intelligence bestowed on her by the gods, possessed a woman's curiosity which unfortunately according to legend proved disastrous. One day when Epimetheus was away, she opened the jar in which Prometheus had collected the evils of the world, among them the knowledge of unavoidable death and misfortune. They escaped before she could close the lid, and man suffered the consequence. Let us also look closely at the nature of the characters in Celaya's vision of reality.

The first character who appears on the scene is Goethe En Off, who is the poet. The *Mono* addresses him: «Eh Señor Poeta!» This character has only two short speeches—one at the beginning and the one at the end of the poem. The poem begins:

Goethe, En Off:

Vosotros, aquí abajo, sentís lo deseable,
mas lo que debe ser lo saben allí arriba.
Vosotros, titanescos, acometéis lo grande,
mas llevar a lo eterno del bien y la belleza
es obra de los dioses. Confiad sólo en ellos. [2]

The poem ends:

Goethe, En Off:

Tan perdurable soy como los mismos dioses.
Eternos somos todos. No recuerdo mi origen

---

[2]   Gabriel Celaya, *Dos Cantatas* (Madrid: Revista de Occidente, 1964), p. 15.

y no estoy destinado a terminar, ni mi fin veo.
¡Así que soy eterno, pues que soy![3]

Celaya's ideal of the poet is clearly seen in these two statements. The last statement reveals most sharply the poet's ideal nature: As a bringer of the word or understanding he is a prophet; and since the word or understanding will live on through eternity, and because the poet lives for and through his cause, he feels and actually becomes as everlasting as it is:

«Tan perdurable soy como los mismos Dioses.»

The ideal poet is conscious and has gained understanding and freedom. He can choose. Like Quijote he chooses faith in man's immortality.

«Eternos somos todos.»

He states his reason for faith in his most truthful, simple, beautiful, poetic manner:

«No recuerdo mi origen.»

Since he does not remember his origin (his birth) he can choose to believe he has always existed. Moreover since he cannot foresee his termination or death, he can consider himself immortal. There are two levels of interpretation intended here. One is that the poet is immortal through his word; the other infers that this act of faith, this positive attitude, actually serves as a catalyst to start man on his path to awareness and consciousness.

«Así que soy eterno, pues que soy.»

The opening stanza is a statement of the poet's view of mankind, his position and needs. He describes his sleeping state by reference to the limitations of feeling and understanding:

Vosotros, aquí abajo, sentís lo deseable,
Mas lo que debe ser lo saben allí arriba.

---

[3] *Ibid.*, p. 77.

The poet then is a kind of mediator between man and the gods. The kind of service he renders reminds one of Plato's description of love as a mediator between man and the gods. He does not deny man's dignity. «Vosotros, tita-nescos, acometéis lo grande.» But to reach his potential, the maximum of good and beauty, is a work for gods. Men can be nearer or farther from this ideal pattern.

> Mas llevar a lo eterno del bien y la belleza
> es obra de los dioses. Confiad sólo en ellos.

The next character to appear on the stage is *Mono* (representative of Epime-theus), who is suspicious of the poet's words and reminds him of how many ways the same words can and are interpreted. *El Mono* is negative, a skeptic, a doubter.

> ¡Eh, señor poeta!,
> así hablaba también Hitler
> de su estrella.
> Porque todos los tiranos creen en la Providencia
> hasta que les entierran.[4]

But immediately after he doubts he changes and remembers he does not really know anything. He is not conscious:

> ¿O seré yo también
> un tirano que dicta según su inconsciencia?[5]

Then he changes again and justifies his not knowing—or at least tries to:

> ¡Ay, no! Yo formo parte
> —vean, vean—
> del carnaval real de la vida animal.

At least he is not completely unaware of his present animal-like state. He uses his knowledge for the wrong reasons however. His negative attitude toward himself and all around him keep him from using the latent power that all men

---

[4] Gabriel Celaya, *Dos Cantatas*, p. 15.
[5] Gabriel Celaya, *Dos Cantatas*, p. 15.

possess, and keep him in a state of inertia.

The next entrance is made by *Zomorros*, the sons of *Ingeniero*, who represent humanity. *Zomorros*, as Celaya explains, is a type of terrifying mask of animal faces used in Basque carnivals. Their animal-like nature in the poem is made overwhelmingly evident. Their first sounds are not words but animal-like cries: *Huj, huj, huj,* and their life is one of misery and enslavement to their own base nature. Celaya's idea of man as machine, possessing no control over himself or his attitudes before he gains consciousness, is evidenced most clearly in the depiction of these characters. Their opening statement shows the various sides of the predicament:

> ¡ Huj, huj, huj ! Rastrear la miseria. Hozar en lo real.
> Bestias, no, no pensamos. Balbucimos. **Aullamos,**
> sumidas en lo espeso de la vida indistinta.
> ¡ ayayay ! ¡ A-i ! ¡ Huj ! Lloramos nuestra rabia
> y rasgamos el raso de la noche luciente.
> Algo que es sólo instinto, gemido, luz raspante,
> aullido de victoria vital y a un tiempo muerte,
> o bien melancolía, porque todo se alarga
> y aunque nada pronuncia parece que trasciende
> —¡ huj, jurujú, huj, huj !—como un calor se siente.
> y antes de las palabras, ese sabor de origen
> y ese inarticulado chocar con la rompiente,
> denuncia, aunque no enuncia, toda la opacidad.
> Si alguien nos escuchara, cabría decir algo,
> pero basta un aullido frente a lo indiferente,
> y es tan sólo una risa mecánica y salvaje,
> y es tan sólo el murmullo mortal de la corriente,
> y es tan rara y tan baja la materia en que estamos,
> y es tan poco el estado, dado por suficiente,
> en que nos prolongamos, casi nos entendemos
> fundidos uno en otro como un barro sagrado
> que articular palabras es aceptar la muerte.[6]

They admit they are beasts and do not think but only track misery—root like hogs in reality, howl and stammer. The movement of the verse emphasized by the yells, punctuation and monotonous anaphoristic repetition of «y»

---

[6] Gabriel Celaya, *Dos Cantatas*, p. 16.

and «y es» at the beginnings of lines gives the reader the feeling that though these words are being spoken they are only imitated and mouthed and not really understood by the speakers. Although they live the reality, they do not demonstrate true understanding coming from thought and decision. These creatures are even more negatively oriented than *Mono*. One sees in them the idea of life as a dream not really lived at all:

>«Porque todo se alarga
>y aunque nada pronuncia *parece que* trasciende»[7]
>. . . . . : . . . .
>y ese inarticulado chocar con la rompiente,
>denuncia, aunque no enuncia, toda la opacidad.[8]

Los Zomorros:

>. . . . .
>Mas ¿no eres tú también un simio, una apariencia,
>un loco ante un espejo donde no es él quien surge,
>sino un fantasma extraño? Mono, Mono, eres mono.[9]

The awareness of death, the ultimate consequence of existence, brings their complete and total despair:

>y es tan poco el estado, dado por suficiente,
>en que nos prolongamos, casi nos entendemos
>fundidos uno en otro como un barro sagrado
>que articular palabras es aceptar la muerte.[10]

That they do not possess consciousness is stated in exactly those terms:

>pero si nos quitaran la máscara sagrada
>tendríamos conciencia, daríamos el paso
>que tú, mono estás dando sin saber dónde irrumpes.[11]

---

[7] *Ibid.*
[8] Gabriel Celaya, *Dos Cantatas*, p. 16.
[9] *Ibid.*, p. 17.
[10] *Ibid.*, p. 16.
[11] *Ibid.*, p. 17.

Mono indeed can articulate it even more clearly:

El Mono:

. . . . . .
Todos vivimos dormidos,
unos más,
otros menos,
y despertar
es ver por fin sin velos
lo real. [12]

Mono himself is on his way to consciousness. He has taken the first step which is awareness of his animal-like nature. He has recognized the differences between himself and the Zomorros and his brother, the Engineer.

The next character enters the drama only in voice and is called La Voz de Ezbá. Ezbá is a Basque word meaning, literally translated, «no-sí.» And it was because of this, Celaya explains, that he chooses it to represent the feminine voice of the cantata. Ezbá, through whose voice Pandora whispers, is indeed felt in her totality; she is all passions or all gifts. She sings and speaks of love:

Cantaré. Cantaré.
La rama en flor del manzano
para ti, para mí.
La nube, alegre de abril
para mí, para ti. [13]

She promises happiness:

Las olas del mar querido
para ti, para mí, para el sí
de los corazones que brincan
con el chistu y el tamboril. [14]

---

[12] Ibid., p. 58.
[13] Gabriel Celaya, Dos Cantatas, p. 23.
[14] Ibid., p. 24.

In *Ezbá*'s third speech the release of the evils from Pandora's box is symbolized dramatically by the release of birds. Celaya's use of onomatopoeia here is extremely effective; one can almost hear the whirl of bird wings in the Basque words.

Txori, txoriyá,
txori choruá.
Los pájaros cantan
y Dios se calla.
Los pájaros cantores
que no cantan amores,
cantan sólo por cantar
sin más ni más
Txori, txoriyá,
txori choruá.
Y Dios se calla.
Quizás no haya
que decir nada. [15]

The first two lines of the stanza are Basque and may be translated into Spanish as *los pájaros — los pájaros locos.*

One feels the symbolic nature of *Ezbá* more strongly than that of any of the other characters. She is not real. She does not even appear personally in the poem; only her voice is heard: *la voz de Ezbá.*

Ezbá, like the other characters, feels the victimization or inevitibality of her position in the world. She, too, is wistful and melancholy. She realizes that the loss caused by her lack of awareness was as surely hers as it was everyone's:

Pajarillos, reíd,
cantad, cantad.
Los vi venir
mas no fue así.
Los vi volar
allá, allá.
Abrí la mano;
cerré. Y en vano.

---

[15] Gabriel Celaya, *Dos Cantatas*, p. 29

Nada he cazado.
Pajarrillos perdidos
¡a la gloria, a la gloria!
Tenía uno cogido
y escapó. ¿Para qué?
¡Qué más da!
Pajarillos, ¡volad!
No os dejéis explicar. [16]

Her nature is love but unawareness caused her to prove a greater evil than good for mankind. In spite of the grace and beauty bestowed upon her by the gods, Curiosity, the tragic flaw devised by Zeus, betrayed her into opening the box in which man's suffering lay dormant, imprisoned with the ills of disease and death; only hope did not escape. In the poem by Celaya *Mono* expresses clearly the two sides of her true nature.

Ven tú, amorosa, ven como la noche crece,
deseo sin objeto, tú que eres el no-objeto
y el placer imposible que en el límite busca
imposibilidades. ¡Ay, no tú, Ezbá, no-sí,
sí, ven, Ezbá, indecisa, transparente, inasible,
temblorosa de luces, soñadora, engañosa. [17]

She is the embodiment of the paradox, the fusion of *no-sí*—the duality synthesized in one:

Que sí, que sí,
que en los pulsos me salta
tú no que sí.
Que no, que no.
Te pensaré a lo lejos,
mas vete, amor. [18]

Que no, que sí,
Que en los dentros me baila

[16] Gabriel Celaya, *Dos Cantatas*, p. 36.
[17] *Ibid.*, p. 65.
[18] *Ibid.*, p. 65.

algo sin fin.
Que sí, que no,
contra ti, contra mí,
soy dos. [19]

Nevertheless, in spite of the ills she brought to mankind as the mother of women her nature is love. She seeks to give it as well as receive it. Celaya, for the most part, presents her in a sympathetic light, as the suffering she brings is necessary for man's enlightenment. Even if love is unattainable because of her own nature, she seeks after it. Like Prometheus she finds revolt:

> ¡Si supieras, Ingeniero...!
> Volvía, me revolvía,
> y era igual.
> Vivía toda mi vida
> para mal.
> Ni comía, ni bebía,
> ¡ayayay!
> ¡Si supieras, Ingeniero...!
> Ni tan siquiera podía
> respirar.
> Por mi amor, ay, por mi amor
> nada más.
> Por sus ojos que no ven
> al brillar.
> ¡Si supieras, Ingeniero...!
> En esa luz que va y viene,
> muero yo.
> Ni se nota cuando digo:
> Aquí estoy.
> Ingeniero... [20]

Ingeniero however cannot love the inconsistent (*Ezbá*) with the same fervor as his work. He recognizes *Ezbá* in her true nature, and although his own solitude makes the statement more painful, he explains her nature and what one's attitude toward her is to be if man is to win as much as he can

---

[19] *Ibid.*, p. 56.
[20] Gabriel Celaya, *Dos Cantatas*, p. 64.

which is to awake:

Ezbá, ¿quién es Ezbá? Un ave ausente.
Ezbá, ¿dónde está Ezbá? En lo evidente.
Es real, luminosa, transeúnte,
no existe si se ofrece, mas se muestra
cuando escapa volando libremente.
Conozco esa falacia de los dioses
que Ezbá, como Pandora a Prometeo,
os propone, hijos míos, niños míos.
¡Tan bella! Sí, lo sé, tan deseable
que cabe disculpar vuestro delirio
pensando que en su voz se hace un fantasma,
y el fantasma, presencia obsesionante,
y en tanto que no existe, doblemente.
¡Ezbá! ¿Quién es Ezbá, forma del humo,
equívoca, ligera, mentirosa,
hija y madre a la vez, amante siempre,
voluble, soñadora, caprichosa?
Algo que debería daros miedo
por gratuito, falaz e inconsistente,
tan bello sin razón y no debido,
que cabe sospechar alguna trampa
ante tanto regalo derramado.
Por eso yo quisiera que pensarais.
Los hombres somos hombres decididos,
arrancados al sueño de una hondura
terrible, poderosa y fascinante.
Quizás simples y toscos, quizás niños,
si pensamos lo inmenso de un pasado
que no cabe evocar y sin embargo
perdura opacamente y nos retrasa
en el seno terrible de las Madres.
¡Alcemos el orgullo de estrenarnos!
Si nacimos de un sueño femenino,
somos la desnudez y la alegría
lanzadas limpiamente a la aventura.
Si venimos de lejos, renunciamos
a las madres piadosas, las esposas,

29

las hijas, las amantes, las hermanas
eróticas, y crueles, y espantosas,
como míticos monstruos naturales.
Pensad que la mujer es algo arcaico,
y nosotros, sus niños indefensos,
tenemos que luchar contra su magia,
su encanto, su envoltura y su mentira.[21]

The *Ingeniero* is the final character to enter into Celaya's dramatic
poem. He is what his title indicates and his ancestor Prometheus would have
been proud of: a builder, a creator out of chaos, an artist, a maker of men.
The lesson was one he learned from the experience of «Creating himself,» as
is explained in Plato's «generation of opposites.» Because of the machine-like
nature of the body and the miraculous touch of fire of the gods, the mind,
man has the opportunity to learn to use his machine, to awaken it in order to
look on life. However, the battle is not an easy one. One must find the paths
little by little and then make one's way slowly up them. One of the principal
paths in this struggle is understanding and using the gift of language. This
idea is closely related to Celaya's ideas on the poet's place in the modern
world.[22] He says of language:

¡Basta ya de canciones! El lenguaje
es un don prometeico. Agradecedlo
y no lo prolonguéis en ecos vanos.
Hablar es concertar, buscar acuerdo,
dirigirse a los otros y ordenarnos.
Las voces de trabajo son consignas
que nos hacen a todos solidarios.
A veces es bastante decir sólo:
«¡Ale, ya, dad, eup!», pues nos une.
Por eso los martillos cuando suenan,
las hoces cuando siegan, los motores
cuando marchan y alientan casi humanos,
puntúan esos ritmos populares
que no son los que tú estás masturbando.
El hombre que habla solo no está hablando.

---

[21] Gabriel Celaya, *Dos Cantatas*, pp. 69-70.
[22] See Chapter IV.

El hombre que se queja no es un hombre.
Aúlla, sólo aúlla, no articula,
y es un mono, sí, Mono, sólo un mono.[23]

His solution is ultimately practical and simple. One must work. One must solve the daily problems of living: food and shelter and order. This is at least the first step in the solution:

¿Qué falsa religión o qué nihilismo
intentas predicarnos, viejo Mono?
No quiero replicarte en las alturas
o yendo por las ramas a tu gusto.
Pretendo resolver urgentemente
los pequeños problemas de mis hijos.
Necesitan comer, necesitan un orden,
una ley y una Polis que los salven
de la vida selvática en que yacen.
Sólo cuando resuelvan sus problemas
más simples y más arduos verán claro
qué estúpido es tu cuento de belleza
en las mil y una noches de tus nanas.
Trabajemos. Montemos otro mundo
en el que tengan todos lo preciso:
Alimento, una casa, unos vestidos.
Busquemos soluciones, no respuestas
a superferolíticos problemas.
Ya sé —no me repliques—, las cuestiones
materiales no son las importantes.
Pero son las primeras. Y es posible
que si las resolvemos, tus preguntas
aún sin hallar respuesta, ya no surjan,
se desvanezcan, sí, dejen de hacerse.[24]

Celaya's profound concern and love for humanity and *Los de abajo* is evident. He feels that once the material needs are eliminated, spiritual progress becomes possible.

---

[23] Gabriel Celaya, *Dos Cantatas*, pp. 33-34.
[24] Gabriel Celaya, *Dos Cantatas*, pp. 35-36.

31

Through depiction of the personalities of these characters Celaya describes what he believes to be that part of man's nature that keeps him from consciousness as well as those undeveloped possibilities which can lead him in that direction if he becomes aware of them. A man, of couse, never struggles after something he believes he already possesses, and this is perhaps the key to the whole situation. Man must realize what he is now, his mechanicalness and suffering, as well as what he can become, before he will have sufficient desire and understanding to escape. Speaking to *Los Zomorros, Mono* states:

> Sois reyes encantados.
> Sois príncipes antiguos y futuros.
> Una conciencia pulsa
> tras vuestros mascarones animales.
> ¡Sois tanto! No sabéis.
> Sois monstruos sin palabras.
> No seres sin angustia iluminante,
> sino dioses dudosos.
> Sois el hombre anticipado,
> y yo como vosotros.[25]

Consciousness pulsates behind their animal faces. Man is a paradox himself: an animal in form capable of becoming a God (Sois reyes encantados, Dioses dudosos).

The chief factor that keeps man from this development seems to be lying —particularly lying to himself about himself. He becomes a creature of illusions.

Mono:

> Fabulador. Comediante.
> Imitador de aquello que aún no existe.
> Imitador de todo.[26]

He is nothing in reality; he only imitates.

---

[25]   Gabriel Celaya, *Dos Cantatas*, p. 19.
[26]   *Ibid.*, p. 18.

Mono:

Juego al ser que no soy,
me desdoblo, salto,
me vuelvo de prisa mirando hacia atrás
y me asombro siempre de que allí lejos, nadie
me advierta intempestivo,
peligroso,
o bien, digamos, distinto.[27]

Zomorros:

Somos bestias alegres, feroces, transeúntes
que bailan la inconsciencia. . . .[28]

Zomorros speaking to *Mono*:

. . . . y que salvan
a la vez nuestra vida de esos encantamientos
en los que, sin ser, somos algo casi real.[29]

The distinguishing characteristic of the nature of unconscious beings is their lack of self-control. They are moved to act by external forces rather than internal ones. They do not exist; they are caused to exist. *Mono* describes this situation as imitation. But the *Zomorros*, who are even less advanced, describe it as *encantamiento* in whose power they are, without actually being, something almost real.

Another feature that keeps man from consciousness is his lack of unity. Because of his imitative nature, his tendency to identify and lose himself in all, and his illusions or dreams of himself, his nature or self is divided, not simply once but into a thousand different «I's» heading in their separate directions.

Still another characteristic of man's nature that keeps him from moving forward in a direct line into consciousness is his inertia, his perpetual habit of

---

[27] Gabriel Celaya, *Dos Cantatas*, p. 18.
[28] *Ibid.*, p. 20.
[29] *Ibid.*

flowing with the current, to do the thing that requires the least energy and effort:

Los Zomorros:

¡A la huelga, a la huelga! ¡Viva las cero horas!
Matemos las semanas de color indistinto.
Porque todo es gratuito, porque siempre es domingo
si en verdad nuestra vida desbarata la inercia.[30]

Los Zomorros:

¡A-í! ¡Ah! ¡Oh! ¡Ah, ah! Tiremos la herramienta,
crucémonos de brazos, vivamos el silencio
en el que todo, limpio, vuelve a ser lo que era.
¿Para qué trabajar? ¿Para quién trabajamos?
¿Qué riega este sudor de unas horas vacías
en que damos y damos sin saber lo que hacemos?
Vivir es una fiesta: Un hecho extraordinario
que sería locura enterrar en constancias.
¡A la fiesta! ¡A la huelga! ¡A lo libre, a lo bello!
¡Ayayay! ¡Huj, huj! ¡Raj! ¡Viva el ocio sagrado![31]

The *Ingeniero*, who has gained consciousness, recognizes the error of the *Zomorros*' way and tries to motivate them and bring them to understanding. Consciousness requires effort.

¡Cobardes! ¡Desgraciados! ¡Hijos míos!
¿Otra vez en holganza? ¡Vamos, vamos!
¿Qué hacéis? ¿Estáis soñando? ¡Ale! ¡Eup!
Ocupad vuestros puestos de trabajo,
empuñad la herramienta, golpead,
dad y dad a compás, todos unidos,
el ritmo que edifica nuestro mundo:
Un refugio salvado del capricho
de los dioses antiguos. Levantemos

---

[30] Gabriel Celaya, *Dos Cantatas*, p. 25.
[31] *Ibid.*, pp. 29-30.

con el fuego secreto y prometeico
y una técnica nueva nuestra aurora.

Golpead, vamos, dad con el martillo
y el puño bien cerrado la protesta
de todos los alzados contra el Hades.
Vamos a edificar un mundo humano,
humano, sólo humano, limitado,
y en él hallaréis todos finalmente
la luz y la alegría sin destino.
¡Vamos! ¡Dad! ¡Al trabajo! ¿Listos? ¡Ya!
¿Por qué no miráis quietos? ¿Estáis locos?[32]

Esclavo de sus obras, vuestro padre
es hijo de sus hijos ciertamente.
Mas no puedo admitir vuestro abandono.
Yo quisiera quereros, pero como
perdonar la torpeza repetida?[33]

Inertia or lack of power to do seems to stem from a certain negative attitude which manifests itself in various ways; sadness or melancholy is one of them. A certain perverse satisfaction seems to be found in suffering and self pity. It is of course rationalized. The following speech of *Mono's* is a good example of the consistency of these feelings and the ways they are rationalized:

Yendo y volviendo,
si yo contara...
Lo vivo todo.
No creo en nada.
Al fin encuentro
una sonrisa;
¡Oh tú, mi antigua
melancolía!
Una dulzura
que me acaricia
sin conocerme:

---

32 Gabriel Celaya, *Dos Cantatas*, p. 30.
33 *Ibid.*, p. 31.

Melancolía.
Una distancia
que no distingo:
Melancolía.
¡Melancolía,
dorado otoño,
azúcar negro,
zumo de vida!
Atardeceres,
¡tanto anduvimos!
La brisa pasa
lenta y lenta, larga.
¡Si yo contara!
¡Melancolía!
¿O es la belleza?
Vivo una pausa.
Pues bien pensado,
no pasa nada,
y bien vivido,
todo es perfecto,
indiferente.
¡Está tan lejos![34]

This negativeness, inertia, self-delusion, and lack of unity and understanding keep man from living in the present moment, which is of course the only real one. He either looks to the past or the future, usually the former because of these mechanical habits. The idea of the eternal present, the beauty of the moment, is expressed through *Mono*:

Un momento vivaz
es lo que es.
Lo demás
queda en hablar por hablar.
¿Qué podemos añadir
de verdad
a las cosas que ya están
en su momento puntual?

---

[34] Gabriel Celaya, *Dos Cantatas*, pp. 32-33.

Lo real ¡es tan real!
En el temblor
del zarzal
queda el pájaro que ha huido;
en el árbol, la forma
aún vivible del viento
que duda y pasa,
mintiéndose, siguiendo.
Nada permanece. Todo vive.
El momento es lo total.
¿Y qué?
Nada. Nada más.
El sonido del agua,
la fragancia del otoño,
el tordo que se dispara
y trita solo.
Así, sentado,
sin hacer nada,
callo porque el mundo
es inmenso y está quieto.[35]

¡Idiotas! Sí que viene
naciendo del deseo y el origen del mundo,
aún borboteante.
Mas no es lo que se puede
sujetar abrazando,
agotar poseyendo.
¡Mirad!, es la belleza, tan sólo la belleza.
Un cuerpo libre; un hecho
indemne que resbala por la nada,
un momento libre,
y evidente, increíble,
que niega la ceguera del instinto
como un dios pasajero
que insulta, en cuanto existe, a los Eternos.
Mirad, es el momento,
nada más, nada menos

---

[35] Gabriel Celaya, *Dos Cantatas*, pp. 24-25.

que instantáneo y perfecto.
¡Mirad! ¿Lo veis? Ya es otro. Lo ha retratado el cielo.[36]

But the difficulty involved in keeping this awareness as well as the consequence in thought when it is lost is also expressed vividly in *Mono*:

Es muy fácil anunciar,
más difícil suspender
lo que arrastra y pensar que...
No sé. No sé.
No coincido exactamente
con el momento en que vivo.
Hay algo que me remueve
¿para qué?
Soy el resto decimal
que tras mil operaciones
se acostumbra despreciar.
No soy quién.
¿Y si fuera prehumano?
¿Y si fuera posthumano?
¿Y si el hombre aún no existiera
de veras, qué?[37]

Besides ridding oneself of old habits which are detrimental, one must have added certain things.

In order to free oneself and come to a right understanding which can lead to consciousness, many steps must be taken and all require efforts, indeed super efforts.

El Ingeniero:

. . . .
Mas no podréis vivir sin esforzaros.
Ni siquiera vivir como animales.
Mirad a los obreros constructivos
que erigen en la nada su esperanza,

---

[36] *Ibid.*, p. 22.
[37] Gabriel Celaya, *Dos Cantatas*, p. 40.

respiran con el ritmo del trabajo,
y se hacen quienes son, edificando
a la vez que su ser, lo colectivo.
Sed limpios. Sed audaces. Mirad claro
qué inmenso es lo posible a nuestro alcance.
A veces derrotados, no humillados,
a veces—¡cuántas veces!—explotados
pero heroicos y duros contra todo,
alzando el desafío y la nobleza
de los no resignados, de los altos
hijos de un Prometeo atormentado,
sentimos que luchando nos hacemos
quienes somos de veras poco a poco.[38]

He urges *Zomorros* to think of the great opportunities within their reach if they will only try. He reminds them of their obligation to remember their heritage and the slow labor-filled path that has brought them to the point where they presently find themselves (los altos hijos de un Prometeo atormentado).

First man must separate himself from the mass—from the things he knows to lead away from his aim:

. . . hay que separarse del coro y lo latente,
salvaje y amoroso
y estar en verdad solo
para entender aquello que no puede decirse:
Lo humano y más que humano de los hombres.
Hay que ser un fusilado
por la luz grande de nadie
y crecerse sin embargo.
¡Ay!, hablo demasiado.
Un mono, ya se sabe,
que es algo peligroso, dudosamente sano.
Un mono es como un hombre en sus principios.

---

[38] *Ibid.*, pp. 46-47.

Si vive de verdad sólo vive de excesos,
aunque es redondo el silencio.[39]

The idea of sacrifice on the part of those who have come before is emphasized here again by a reference to those who died in the Spanish civil war.
One is reminded particularly of Lorca (Hay que ser un fusilado/ por la luz
grande de nadie/ y crecerse sin embargo).

This stanza also emphasizes that one must realize his own infinitesimal
position in the vast scheme of things, and not be despaired by it. Celaya's
principal idea, however, is the idea of effort. One must work. Nothing good
is free; it all must be paid for; particularly consciousness, because of its very
nature it must be earned.

The *Ingeniero* who plays the role of Prometheus is constantly aware of
the idea of payment. The latter paid a very high price for the fire he stole for
mankind. He was a God and was consequently not unaware that his punish-
ment would be severe—yet he agreed to pay because he loved sufficiently to
be willing. The close parallel with Jesus is evident. The principal of payment
is well known in the Bible also, specifically the New Testament.

Thus it is the *Ingeniero* who expresses the idea of effort or payment being necessary for true life or for consciousness:

Las voces de trabajo son consignas
que nos hacen a todos solidarios.[40]

One must remember that life is a paradox and change. This is man's one
hope. The past is not absolute. It is only the backdrop of today against which
one must shape his future. The past can be changed by changing today. But
one must change with effort. One must pay. One must understand the
mystery of being a man and accept effort and suffering willingly. It is precisely
this acceptance of suffering and refusing to be cast into negativeness and inertia that makes the difference, and creates the possibility of consciousness.
Man can then use his full potential for development, and reach his limit in the
image of God.

El Ingeniero:

---

[39] Gabriel Celaya, *Dos Cantatas*, p. 19.
[40] Gabriel Celaya, *Dos Cantatas*, p. 33.

¿No entiendes mi verdad? ¡Es tan sencilla!
Hablas como si el hombre no cambiara
y fuera hoy como ayer, y siempre el mismo.
Pero tú y mis Zomorros levantando
furia y melancolía, ardor sagrado,
postración absoluta, rabia indemne,
tierra y agua de origen, energía
que cambia con la llama no tocable,
y distancias también, cuando abre el viento
con hojas palpitantes lo que espera,
sabéis qué acelerado marcha el mundo.
¿Cómo podría el hombre ese proyecto,
cómo podría yo, cómo tú mismo,
creer que es absoluto su pasado?
No somos lo que fuimos. Lo sabemos.
Y aunque nada supieramos, los pulsos
de origen forzarían nuestro cambio.
Me alcé contra los dioses. Robé el fuego.
Pequé. No me arrepiento. Me mandaban
contra mí mismo aquellos que hoy me niegan.
Comprended el misterio de ser hombres.
Aceptad el orgullo y la miseria.
Nos alzamos terribles, transtornamos
el orden de lo eterno, y con soberbia
yo digo al levantaros: Somos otros.
Otros que, comprended, apenas somos
todavía mas muy pronto seremos.
Otros, contra naturaleza, sólo humanos,
otros, con su justicia, sus ciudades
y sus mil invenciones aún en marcha,
otros, contra el destino de los dioses,
poderosos y alegres, siempre nuevos
hasta la conversión no prevenida
de la naturaleza en artificio.
No somos quienes fuimos. No seremos
nada hasta que aceptemos el trabajo
que ha de hacernos quien somos: Hombres-dioses.[41]

---

[41] Gabriel Celaya, *Dos Cantatas,* pp. 38-39.

He is not unaware, however, that he is what he is only because *Mono* and the others are what they are. *Mono* also recognizes this. Plato's idea of the generation of opposites is obvious:

El Ingeniero:

Tan sucio es lo animal de los comienzos,
tan lento el progresar del hombre nuevo,
tan espesa la masa de que quiero
extraer a mis hijos prometeicos
que a veces desespero. Y cuando miro
en ti, Mono, a mi hermano preferido,
no puedo despreciarte, pues sería
despreciarme a mí mismo en mis principios
y en algo que en mí dura no resuelto.
Porque, hermano, es verdad, te llevo dentro
y cuando te combato, me combato
a mí mismo con ira, y no sería
tan tajante la rabia con que lucho
si no fuera yo mismo mi enemigo.[42]

El Mono:

Nadie sin su contrario
es quien es, hermano.
Sin el no ser del ser
lo real no es real.[43]

El Ingeniero:

¡Ah, los espejos! ¡Ah, los mil espejos!
¿Qué doblez de conciencia me convierte
en un ser desprendido y falseado
que no cree en lo que dice y se sospecha
fantasma entre otros seres incompletos?
Doblez. ¡Todo es doblez! Aspecto solo.

---

[42] Gabriel Celaya, *Dos Cantatas*, p. 54.
[43] *Ibid.*

Falacia necesaria. Fabulosa
mentira y a la vez realidad.
Yo daría un total contigo, Mono,
porque eres mi gemelo y mi contrario
como yo soy el tuyo, si y no, sino,
mas tú te quieres Mono, mono y solo.
¡Ay! ¿Quién tendrá la llave de esta trampa?
Mi técnica y tu magia son lo mismo.
tu sueño y mi combate, igual locura,
y tú cuando renuncias, respirando
la paz del ancho mundo, llevas dentro
la lucha que yo pongo siempre fuera
mientras dentro de mí se abre la nada.[44]

Darwin's theory of man's evolution from the primates is reaffirmed and carried further. Man as we know him in the twentieth century can evolve, but
the evolution is no longer physical but psychological instead. Some men
have evolved but only a few.

¿creer que es absoluto su pasado? no somos
lo que fuimos ... ... Somos otros.
Otros que, comprended, apenas somos
todavía mas muy pronto seremos.[45]

The interweaving of the various levels of myth and variations of reality
gives extraordinary results. The complete experience of Celaya's ideas comes
to the fore without impairing their complexity. Will = Consciousness. Consciousness means will and will means freedom. In life aim is the correlating
factor—exemplified in the *Zomorros* and *Ingeniero*. What is the difference
between them? Their aim. This one thing produces the kind of action they
must take. Hope, or Pandora's last gift in Goethe's version of the legend, is
the one left with which Prometheus the engineer found meaning, and
learned to make of himself the very most possible.

Zomorros really have no aim. They are too negative and confused to
have a single long-viewed aim. But Prometheus is the Creator, an *ingeniero*
—he can not be satisfied without a long range aim. The best one he can im-

---

[44] *Ibid.*, pp. 57-58.
[45] Gabriel Celaya, *Dos Cantatas*, p. 39.

agine he makes every effort to fulfill. He hopes to awaken man to his responsibility, to point him in the proper direction for the improvement of man's position. Since they have not reached his level of insight, he attempts to guide them. But at the same time he realizes a certain limitation because he has within him some of the traits he hopes to correct. The mirror reflects oneself in all the complexity of this dual nature: one part *sí*, one part *no*. Thus the anguish of the *Ingeniero* and also the poet. A rebirth to consciousness is desirable for the poet also because he, like the *Ingeniero*, still has traits of the *Mono* (te llevo dentro), and when he contemplates himself he sees paradoxically the *sí* and the *no*. He must struggle (a dynamic concept) against the *no* part of his existence, the *Mono*. Thus there are several levels or traits in humanity and in each individual, from the lowest (*Zomorros*) to the second stage (*Mono*) to the highest (*Ingeniero*). Thus the paradox of rebirth and consciousness.

III
Mysticism

Mysticism, because of its broad application and obscure nature, is difficult to define with exactitude. A brief glance at the etymology as well as a few definitions by outstanding literary critics will shed some light into its obscurity. «The word mystic is derived from the Greek ηνγτιός (mystikos), and the noun ηνγτήριον (mysterion), in the plural ηνγτήρια (mysteria), which means secret doctrines, hidden and secret rites, secret cults.»[1]

It is Celaya's belief that we have a dualistically constructed mind which cannot take in the identity of opposites. What we call the antithesis of opposites exists actually only in our minds—in our subjective view of the world. The poet is mystic in his attempt to approach the absolute: the all, the oneness of things which must include nothing if it is all. «Todo es todo y nada»[2] Celaya exclaims. He understands the dual nature of reality deeply but normal words (no words in our language) can include simultaneously thesis and antithesis. Consequently our minds cannot grasp them as one idea. A very famous mystic, Martin Heidegger, got around this problem most successfully by inventing his own words. One of his most notorious examples is «Das Wesende» which is a past participle of the word Sein, to be, to which a «d» has been added to form it into a present participle. A literal translation: «beening» seems to simply provide a new perspective which reveals a process of «having beeness.» Another example is «Befallenheit» the state of being falling,

---

[1]   David Baumgardt, *Great Western Mystics* (New York: Columbia University Press, 1961), pp. 1-2.
[2]   Gabriel Celaya, *Poesía*, p. 364.

which he uses to describe man's position in the world. «Ausgeworfenheit» the state of being thrown into, is the other dimension or view of the same question. Heidegger's main preoccupation, like Celaya's, was consciousness. He, however, termed it differently: authentic or inauthentic existence. Authentic coincides with consciousness or living each moment as though it were one of few and must be completely filled. This idea also preoccupied the existentialists. Heidegger's example of authentic existence is enlightening. Dostoyevski was sentenced to death and was reprieved but he did not know it until the last minute. This exacted of him, for his own moral conscience, that he live each moment as though it were a lifetime.

Celaya is no less ambitious than Heidegger; he wishes to bring understanding/authentic living to his fellow man. So with the poet's soul of a man dedicated to light and love he invents words, he reshapes meaning, he fuses opposites. He struggles to bring man's mind out of the rigid patterns which in his conception keep him completely unconcious. His poetry recalls immediately some of the Hindu gods which combine complete opposites in themselves.

It is important to note that Buddhism, which is the strongest «religious» influence on Celaya's poetry, in its original and purest form does not profess belief in any supernatural being.

For Celaya as well religion is a way of life, one which leads man to his highest destiny and enables him to overcome both internal and external mechanical forces. From Celaya's point of view mysticism has been, and continues to be misunderstood by ordinary man. Its language is the language of men who have reached a higher level, who have gained more consciousness and therefore it is not understood by ordinary sleeping men. One is led to believe that Celaya does not find the mystic's direct communication with God to be one of interpersonal communication but rather an increased understanding brought on by consciousness which reveals the objective truth of existence and its meaning to the possessor.

It is a fact that the idea of man's obtaining something more for himself, new powers and new understanding, is an old one. It is found primarily in literature, art and religion. Mystics are perhaps the principal spokesmen for these higher states (mystics of many religions and at all times). There seem to be various ways to prepare for these states quite different in nature but all of which lead to the same objective: to obtain higher states of awareness and increased control of oneself. The way of the Fakir, for instance, is a physical way where the objective is reached by learning to conquer physical pain. Another way is the way of the Yoga who uses increased knowledge and understanding. Still another is the religious man or monk who uses faith to obtain his aim.

Celaya nowhere states that he does not believe that these men believed in a personal God, but he illustrates that it is not necessary that they believe in order to gain consciousness or awareness (with, of course, the exception of the religious way). It is only necessary that they live by and believe in the truths they find after having verified for themselves the ways of conduct leading to enlightenment or the higher destiny of man.

What one can hope to gain from consciousness, the transformation, manifests itself on many levels. One advantage is that in higher states of awareness thinking is no longer dualistic. In other words, opposites are no longer contradictory but somehow interrelated parts of a vastly complex whole.

Celaya's attitudes toward God and religion are thus highly complex and equally unorthodox. He is not a Christian in the ordinary sense or as ordinary men understand Christianity. However, he is profoundly religious in that he believes the knowledge gained through certain religions like Christianity and Buddhism is the key to enlightenment, or gaining of self-conscious ness and later objective consciousness and consequently power or control over oneself and to some extent ones circumstances. God to Celaya could be defined as love, understanding, the life force or life principle.

The religious influence on the author's attitude toward man is illustrated in the quotation by Mokshadharma which precedes the long poem called «Lo Demás Es Silencio» which the poet himself told me was his most important work.[3] The quotation reads: «Te voy a comunicar una sentencia sagrada y misteriosa: no hay nada superior al hombre.» The three key words which reveal the author's attitude are *sagrada, misteriosa* and *sentencia.* Sacred immediately evokes a religious feeling—and in connection with man: Christ, Buddha, Mohammed, etc. «Misteriosa» reinforces the idea of sacred used in reference to man because for man to be sacred (or for the belief that he is to be true) it is necessary that one or more such sacred men have existed. The becoming or existence of such men is indeed mysterious; this mysteriousness is consciousness to Celaya. It in all cases has involved certain esoteric doctrines which the men not only lived by, or achieved enlightenment by, but it is also a doctrine which they teach to others as a means for attaining this same elevated state.

It seems to be this quest after the revelation of the mysteries involved in

---

[3]   Private interview with poet in summer of 1965.

the attainment of enlightenment or achieving this sacred state that is Celaya's primary concern. «Sentencia» is representative of the price one pays for such knowledge and being. It is a reminder that one must indeed pay for everything.

Celaya's preoccupations, then, are closely parallel to those of the mystic: he seeks the harmonious sense of unity traditionally called God. He attempts to disclose the unitary nature of ultimate reality. His problem, like that of all mystics regardless of country or century, is the problem of the one and the many. Celaya, however, has reversed the mystic pattern; man, not God, is the end of his search.

Celaya's concern is humanitarian, philosophical, psychological and poetic, but it is expressed in terms of theology, mysticism, and existentialism because of the irrational nature of the truth to which he wishes to give form and meaning. The poet is not so much preoccupied with man and his relationship to God as man and his relationship to himself, to the earth and to his fellow man. The highly mechanistic, militant society of the twentieth century, perhaps more than any other, has isolated man. Fear, too much knowledge, and anxiety have sealed man within himself, they have torn him from the bosom of nature and the happiness of understanding. Evolution and science have clipped the wings of heaven seekers, and the fast tempo of motors and airplanes has hurried people past one another into solitude. It is this situation that Celaya expresses; and like the mystic who believes death of the human body will release the soul which alone can unite with God, Celaya believes that with the death of the human body, the breaking of the isolating walls of the self, the soul of man can unite with all elements of the universe and become «nada y todo,» man's original state:

Todo espera tranquilo y soy yo mismo muerto,
yo mismo que he olvidado lo que fui, que reposo
sobre esta dulce ausencia de no sentirme nada,
que es un sentirme todo, que es no sentirme a mí.[4]

This idea of the contradiction of true existence, that in order to live we must annihilate the self, is repeated again and again with extraordinarily vivid imagery, both traditional and modern:

Así vivo flotando, flotando sin sentido,

---

[4]   Gabriel Celaya, *Poesía*, p. 29.

viviendo con la luz, con la tierra y la luz,
obediente a su impulso, negando mi existencia,
matándome o buscando una vida total.[5]

todo esto quiero, lo valiente, ligero,
abrasado, veloz, limpio de ciegas
y densas somnolencias vegetales,
libre de la pasiva pesadez de la carne siempre inerte.[6]

The poet actually states more than once that life is contradiction; one simply does not exist without it:

... de saber que estoy vivo
y que me contradigo para seguirlo estando.
. . . .
Respirar que es ser no siendo:
Irse y venir con el aire:
Contradecirse y vivir
de este doble movimiento.[7]

The idea of ridding the soul of the body, of dying in order to live, is expressed just as the mystics expressed it, but the goal is slightly different, at least in perspective. Celaya's search seems to be more humanitarian and less individual. Breaking free from the self is more than a revelation of divine truth or the salvation of the soul: it is more than comprehension and union with God for the particular individual. It represents the possibility of a spiritual union with one's fellow man, with the earth and nature, of which man was once an integral part. It destroys man's limitations: the chains of time and self which bind him to misery:

... «yo, tú, él, hoy, mañana»,
esto que separa y es dolor sin remedio.[8]

Celaya's mysticism is a search for brotherhood which reflects the possibilities

[5] Gabriel Celaya, *Poesía*, p. 29.
[6] *Ibid.*, p. 43.
[7] *Ibid.*, p. 94.
[8] Gabriel Celaya, *Poesía*, p. 200.

of salvation for the world. He even contemplates the idea of the body as divine matter:

> sentí que era posible salvar el mundo entero,
> salvarme en él, salvarlo, ser divino hasta en cuerpo.[9]

It is only the intermingling of all things that can bring happiness:

> ¡Ay, alegría! Crecer,
> ser y ser, y más ligero,
> en el aire, en el amor,
> ver que todo es cuerpo nuestro.[10]

The duality of man's nature for Celaya is not as simple as the division of spiritual and corporal made by traditional mystics. Modern man's problem is more complex. The easy solutions to man's condition given by the Bible are no longer acceptable; the poet seeks elsewhere for the answers. One is reminded reading the poetry of Celaya of the belief, popularized by D.H. Lawrence, that the primitive myth-maker lies beneath the surface of the supposedly civilized man. This idea of another «self» that inhabits the body is one of Celaya's principal poetic themes. Sometimes it takes the form of the divisibleness of the self—the lack of unity which keeps man from consciousness. The other «self» (lo otro) that man becomes aware of is somehow related to the part of him which is poet, or creator, the part capable of consciousness. That is indicated in several ways. In a poem entitled «Quien me habita,» the first of the collection Soledad Cerrada (1935), the body sits, opens and closes its eyes, listens, repeats its name; but it is the other self that speaks, that jars the body into excitement and life:

> ¡Qué extraño es verme aquí sentado,
> y cerrar los ojos, y abrirlos, y mirar,
> y oír como una lejana catarata que la vida se derrumba,
> y cerrar los ojos, y abrirlos, y mirar!
>
> ¡Qué extraño es verme aquí sentado,
> y agarrarme una mano con la otra,

---

[9] Ibid., p. 221.
[10] Ibid., p. 94.

y tocarme, y sonreír, y decir en voz alta
mi propio nombre tan falto de sentido!

¡Oh, qué extraño, qué horriblemente extraño!
La sorpresa hace mudo mi espanto.
Hay un desconocido que me habita
y habla como si no fuera yo mismo.

The constant repetition of «y» portrays the monotony and mechanical repetitious nature of the body's life. In the last stanza, the discovery of the other self, this device is conspicuously absent, adding movement and force to the lines. The implication is that without this other self, the speaker or creator, man would be intolerably isolated: seated, listening to life crumble, feeling the push of the heart, a caged bird, forcing the blood with difficulty through his veins. This other self is conscious of his own lack of unity and mechanical-like nature.

The ability to speak of the other self is a recurrent symbol throughout the poet's work. In «El espejo» from the same collection the poet describes the release of this inner being whose voice reveals him:

Un fantasma se levanta de mis ruinas congeladas
y soy yo, soy yo mismo, mi doble.
Oigo su voz que es un frío en mis huesos,
su voz que me revela... No sé; no recuerdo. [11]

It is only this inner self that can reveal man's true identity. Like the poet, the other self is capable of comprehension, of taking into itself or becoming part of universal life: suffering, happiness, light, shadow, all the multiple experiences of existence. The negation of one's own life, to a certain extent at least, is a partial requisite for a poet, but in doing so he extends the area of his personality; he becomes more than he was. Celaya expresses precisely such attitudes toward the poet in many poems. He refers, however, to himself and does not use the word poet. The meaning is nevertheless obvious. In a moment of non-creativity the poet laments his loss of the life-giving fire which lent him his ability:

Vuelvo al bosque y en vano animo en mí los trances

---

[11] Gabriel Celaya, *Poesía*, p. 15.

de la vida primera y el terror que me ahondaba.
Algo ha muerto en mi sangre que era, fuerte, mi fuego.
Hoy camino y me paro a mirar un helecho,
cuento distraído los nervios de una hoja,
me fijo en mil detalles por pequeños, absurdos,
que absorben mis momentos consumiéndome en nada.
. . . .
¿Hay algo más grotesco que un hombre preocupado,
que mientras todo cambia—azul, árboles, agua—
pasa absorto buscando solución a problemas
pequeños de su oscuro vivir de cada día?...[12]

In a later poem entitled «A Blas de Otero» the parallel between the inner self, or consciousness, which alone can unite with the universe, and the poet becomes even more explicit. Speaking of Blas de Otero, a contemporary Spanish poet, and of himself he says:

Nuestra pena es tan vieja que quizás no sea humana:
Ese mugido triste del mar abandonado,
ese temblor insomne de un follaje indistinto,
las montañas convulsas, el éter luminoso,
un ave que se ha vuelto invisible en el viento,
viven, dicen y sufren en nuestra propia carne.
. . . .
Mas es el mundo entero quien se exalta en nosotros
y es una vieja historia lo que aquí desemboca.

Speaking of himself as poet in the same poem he says:

Soy creciente: Me muero. Soy materia: palpito
. . . .
Debo salvarlo todo si he de salvarme entero.
Soy coral, soy muchacha, soy sombra y aire nuevo,
soy el tordo en la zarza, soy la luz en el trino,
soy fuego sin sustancia, soy espacio en el canto,
soy estrella, soy tigre, soy niño y soy diamante
que proclaman y exigen que me haga Dios con ellos.

---

[12] Gabriel Celaya, *Poesía*, p. 68.

52

. . . .
Lo real me resulta increíble y remoto.
Hablo aquí y estoy lejos. Soy yo pero soy otro...[13]

Indeed the poet must bear the burden of all the elements of existence. He must flow from the boundaries and limits of the self and become all things, a glorious but painful experience. In the same poem quoted above, Celaya maintains that the poet in man, or the state of consciousness he associates with it, is his only hope—his only means of salvation. Speaking to Blas de Otero he says:

... El poema creció desde tu centro
con un ritmo de salmo, como una voz remota,
anterior a ti mismo, más allá de nosotros.
Y supe—era un milagro—; Dios al fin escuchaba.
. . . .
Y vi que era posible vivir, seguir cantando.
Y vi que el mismo abismo de miseria medía
como una boca hambrienta, qué grande es la esperanza.
Con los cuatro elementos, más y menos que hombre,
sentí que era posible salvar el mundo entero,
salvarme en él, salvarlo, ser divino hasta en cuerpo.[14]

Thus the seeming contradictions of pain and pleasure are reconciled through creativity. Just as death of the self gave life in a more total and elevated form, so the universal pain which the poet must bear gives pleasure through the elevating forces of creative action, and the unity of ultimate reality becomes apparent.

The idea that consciousness or the inner self, released with the destruction of the body which is mechanical in nature, is closely related to the poet or the creator in man, can be further illustrated by the symbol of the moon, which appears consistently in the poems describing the mystic union and release of the soul. In «El espejo» the speaker ascends to the white cathedral of silence which is death «donde la luna es la virgen desnuda que yo adoro.»[15] In «Rapto» (a poem whose subtitle is a quotation from San Juan de la Cruz.

---

[13] *Ibid.*, p., 219.
[14] Gabriel Celaya, *Poesía*, p. 221.
[15] Gabriel Celaya, *Poesía*, p. 17.

«Adónde escondiste amado, y me dejaste con gemido») the poet addresses
the moon:

> ¡Oh virgen, virgen loca, virgen ciega,
> virgen de la poesía que sólo ve hacia dentro...[16]

The moon, a figure long associated with poetic sentiment, becomes a symbol
of poetry or creativity, the divinity with which man seeks union. It is she the
poet loves and ascends to find. It is she he waits for with expectation and
anxiety like an impatient lover:

> En el bosque oscuro de los hombres callados,
> yo velo, te espero con los brazos en cruz.
> Un puño se cierra con la angustia en mi pecho
> y siento que vives, que esta ausencia eres tú.[17]

But like the other feminine characters in Celaya's poetry she is paradoxical:
the absence is her.

It is interesting to note the intermingling of Christian and sensual imagery used in this poem and many others. The poet refers to the moon as the
«naked *virgin* in a white *cathedral* of silence wrapped in a *halo* of violet silver»
(italics mine). Adjectives such as these of course call to mind immediately the
Virgin Mary. The use here of the contradictory image «naked virgin,» refer-
ring somewhat surprisingly to the virgin with what is usually a more earthy,
sensuous adjective, expresses subtly the theological mystery of the virgin
birth; and equally, the intimated union of man with the virgin moon expresses the at once cosmic and terrestrial mystery of the birth of poetry, or
creativity. The essence of both moon and virgin is revealed in the poet's antithesis: «virgin (o luna), estéril perfección.» The moon is like the virgin Mary in
all the connotations of the word: white, pure, untouched by human hands
and therefore incapable of giving birth; and as Mary gave birth to perfection
in the form of Christ, the virgin moon gives birth to perfection in the form of
poetry. Poetry or creativity, in Celaya's own words is the salvation of mankind. It represents tolerance, understanding and vitality, in its attempt to
teach an understanding of them. Once again one notes Celaya's idea of paradox underlying all organic, life-giving phenomena.

---

[16]   *Ibid.*, p. 17.
[17]   *Ibid.*

54

The Christian imagery interwoven with sensuous concepts of physical love found in Celaya's poetry is reminiscent of the poetry of San Juan de la Cruz and Santa Teresa. Celaya's metaphors, however, are more daring and imaginative, more modern in their subtle allusions to the suffering and anxiety often associated with religion. They are in perfect time with the almost inebriating tone of his poetry.

> ¡Virgen crucificada en mis brazos abiertos!,
> Tan íntima que tan solo tu presencia ya me duele.[18]
> . . . .
> Celeste Inmaculada de mis soledades,
> ¡qué viva te sentía dentro de mí mismo!
> Ya casi te veía, lucífaga, profunda,
> tendida bajo el árbol de los escalofríos.[19]

Even as Celaya has complicated the traditional mystic division of man into corporal and spiritual, so has he complicated the process involved in freeing one's soul or inner self from the body. It is fraught with the complexities of modern psychology. The characteristics which most explicitly distinguish Celaya's poetry from the orthodox are to be found here. Celaya's unique concept of introspection as the path to the other self reveals most clearly his ideas on how the split in man occurred, and what must be done to unify him again in an integral creative human nature. Man's nature is not dual because of an original sin from which man must be freed, unless one conceives of original sin as an allegory describing man's unconscious state. Man was simply created a self evolving being which he must learn about and come to control. Until then he is divided, contradictory and negative. Thus, he is alienated from his fellow man:

> Hay algo denso y callado, algo que pesa y vive:
> el sueño de la tierra dormida en nuestra carne;
> pero el hombre lo ignora y vive sin raíces
> porque nunca ha tocado con pie desnudo el suelo.[20]

> Lloro la inocencia perdida para siempre,

---

[18] Gabriel Celaya, *Poesía*, p. 21.
[19] *Ibid.*, p. 23.
[20] *Ibid.*, p. 28.

55

el ansia que los hombres ahora no comprenden,
que llaman dios, amor, belleza, mar, angustia
y aún muchas cosas más sin sentido igualmente.

. . . .

Y lloro el que los huracanes nos espanten
porque su viento gime, y ríe, y amenaza,
y hace muecas a un tiempo grotescas y terribles;
lloro porque nos asusta lo que debió ser tan nuestro...[21]

It is only vision, understanding of oneself, of the things which are truly essential or which are efforts to awaken that can restore man's human identity. It is only at the core of the human center that the truth of life's meaning can be found. It is this core from whence creativity springs, which in its turn welds seeming contradictions into unity and harmony. It is thus the inward path into oneself that can restore man's lost vision of himself as one with the universe:

Su presencia, mi reflejo, me vuelve hacia mí mismo,
me hunde poco a poco en mis céntricos abismos,
me llena hasta esa blanca catedral del Silencio
donde la luna es la virgen desnuda que yo adoro.[22]

All of the mystic experiences and the release of the inner self from the body described in Celaya's poetry are preceded by this turn inward:

así me he ido agotando, volviéndome hacia dentro
por ansia de unos ojos cerrados para siempre.[23]

Insistente me hunde hacia dentro una muerte
que pesa justamente lo mismo que mi cuerpo.[24]

To sum up Celaya's particular mystic approach then, the following points might be kept in mind. One finds in his poetry an underlying similarity and an inter-relatedness in all that exists. This idea seems to stem from the

---

[21] Gabriel Celaya, *Poesía*, p. 39.
[22] *Ibid.*, p. 14.
[23] *Ibid.*, p. 26.
[24] *Ibid.*, p. 42.

Buddhist doctrine of dependent origination. However, it takes its own particular form in Celaya's poetry—a form often used by metaphysical poets of all times both western and oriental. The particular form expresses itself in two ways. First by synthesis of what is outwardly or superficially opposed and secondly by a direct statement of the poet's feeling of oneness with all that exists. Both of these ideas occur consistently throughout his work. They are one of the most distinguishing marks of his poetry.

Celaya, particularly in his later work, ties these ideas to his ideas of consciousness and its attainment. Man is divided and it is this division, this lack of unity that keeps him in a state of unconsciousness in which he is unable to comprehend the unity of things, and their underlying relation to one another. If a thing is connected inseparably with another there is unity. It is this unity he infers exists. Ordinary man, who has not learned the use of his higher powers, is unable to make connections, unable to feel this unity and consequently feels alienated and alone. Man's power to understand is limited even in his most highly developed state, and paradoxically it is only realization of these limitations that can both cause him to develop what he otherwise would not have and bring him as close as he can come to the understanding of this principle of unity.

Man's life and position in Celaya's view is much like that of the men in Plato's allegory of the cave, who are seated with their backs to the light and who see only shadows reflected in front of them instead of realities. Celaya's poetry is a reiteration of these ideas both philosophically and technically. Celaya, however, is a poet first and only then a philosopher, so his presentation is poetic:

«Canta Martillo. Canta tú hasta matarme.
contra mí, sé constante,
hasta hacerme y hacerme notar que poco importo,
y hacerme ver qué poco soy si soy quien se explica
y cómo cuanto existe se vuelve en mí plausible,
y es en mí, sin yo, vida.»[25]

The mystic influences in Celaya's work take another form besides that associated with Christianity and western mystics, namely that of the oriental religions including Hinduism and Buddhism. This influence is without doubt a stronger one in Celaya's poetry than the method of expression and pro-

---

[25] Gabriel Celaya, *Poesía*, p. 271.

gression of thought of the western mystics. In *La Soledad Cerrada*, a volume of early verse, the subtitle is a quotation from the *Upanishad-Brihadayanka*, the world renowned Hindu philosophy.

«En el Origen nada existía sino Atman.
Miró en torno a sí, y sólo se vio a sí mismo.
Entonces tuvo miedo: Por eso el hombre tiene miedo
               cuando está solo.
Después pensó: ¿De qué tener miedo, puesto que nada
               existe sino yo?
Pero estaba triste: Por eso el hombre está triste
               cuando está solo.
Entonces deseó un segundo ser.»

This is the key to the ideas Celaya is trying to express. His theme is identical to that of the Hindus. Both are trying to express the experience of enlightenment, the creation of a *segundo ser*, one as a poet (through metaphor), the other as a Yoga (through explanation).[26] The method of the latter is analytical and logical explanation, an explicit point by point map of the steps to be taken to achieve enlightenment. The method of the poet is metaphorical. He states the concrete detail of the dilemma with a mystical approach: In solitude I am not alone; someone lives within me. Narcissus sees in the water a being that is not «el mismo» he himself the same. He inclines avidly seeking its secret, but to discover it is to enter into death.[27]

In his more philosophic mood his poetry which reveals the same ideas on consciousness again changes poetic vehicle. The level is still mystical, but it is mystical-allegorical.

Escucha, Mono loco, ¿no has pensado
que también yo te llevo en mis **entrañas**,
latente, revulsivo, doloroso,
mas vivo aunque te nieguen mis razones?
¿No has pensado que fueron tus deseos
y tus necesidades delirantes
el motor de mi lucha y mi conquista?

---

[26] D.W. Bose, *The Yoga-Vasistha Ramayana* (Arpulihane, Calcutta, India: Oriental Publishing Co., 1958), pp. 201-204.

[27] Gabriel Celaya, *Poesía*, pp. 14-16.

Mi técnica nació de tu locura.
Quisiste ser ubicuo, tener botas
de siete leguas y ser invisible,
hacer oro el carbón, y luz, el agua,
y quisiste volar, abrir el cielo,
captar lo que no captan tus sentidos,
detener el pasado y conservarlo
a tu disposición en un armario,
quisiste detener el movimiento
o bien acelerarlo. No podías
pedir nada más mágico y difícil.
Pues bien, todo lo tienes. Es el cine,
la radio y el radar, el microscopio,
la máquina electrónica, el Sputnik,
la luz artificial, los aparatos
de un mundo que robamos a los dioses
y ahora es tuyo, tan tuyo como mío,
pues yo no existiría tan siquiera
si no fuera tu sueño, Mono hermano.
¡Ah, los espejos! ¡Ah, los mil espejos!
¿Qué doblez de conciencia me convierte
en un ser desprendido y falseado
que no cree en lo que dice y se sospecha
fantasma entre otros seres incompletos?
Doblez. ¡Todo es doblez! Aspecto solo.
Falacia necesaria Fabulosa
mentira y a la vez realidad.
Yo daría un total contigo, Mono,
porque eres mi gemelo y mi contrario
como yo soy el tuyo, sí y no, sino,
mas tú te quieres Mono, mono y solo.
¡Ay! ¿Quién tendrá la llave de esta trampa?
Mi técnica y tu magia son lo mismo,
tu sueño y mi combate, igual locura,
y tú cuando renuncias, respirando
la paz del ancho mundo, llevas dentro
la lucha que yo pongo, siempre fuera
mientras dentro de mí se abre la nada.[28]

Celaya attempts to an extensive degree to rid these basic ideas of the profusion of value-loaded words which themselves have become an obstacle to understanding. He brings this about most successfully in the poem already analyzed in detail, *El Derecho y el Revés*, by casting these mystical ideas into ordinary or semi-ordinary modern external circumstances—and then partly on the level of allegory. The value-loaded words are held tight in the concrete example of the engineer, the monkey, woman and suffering mankind, actors symbolic of Prometheus, Epimetheus, Pandora, and Prometheus' creations, *Zomorros*, successively. The latter represented the actors of the mystic level; man, monkey, woman, and suffering humanity on the level of allegory; *Ingeniero, Mono, Ezbá* and *Zomorros* on the practical everyday level.

The mystical ideas of existence become by means of this poetic technique neither subjective nor objective, and consciousness equals simply awareness which belongs neither to the subject nor object. This immediately makes an explanation of both views of the nature of mystic experience easier, because what ultimately all the mystical experiences tend to teach and strive for is liberation or freedom from Karma, one's actions. Man becomes free in life through his understanding of reality and allows his Karma to carry itself out. He does what he is fitted to do normally and does not think about it or suffer over it. Thus it is action without an actor—again the paradox.

---

[28] Gabriel Celaya, *Dos Cantatas*, p. 56.

CALL TO ARMS

IV
The Artist in Society

Celaya's ultimate goal in life as a man and a poet is the transformation of society:

> Para salvar la poesía, como para salvar cuanto
> somos, lo que hay que transformar es la sociedad.
> y a esto debemos consagrarnos con todo
> y por de pronto, si damos en poetas, con
> la poesía como arma cargada de futuro. [1]

He is not simply vaguely concerned about its various failings. He believes fervently that in order for man to continue as a living species he must change. The paths in which he is presently directing himself all lead to destruction. The state of modern man and the twentieth century in Celaya's mind parallels the idea of Einstein, who stated that it was characterized by a perfection of means and a confusion of goals. Mankind has become older and more and more complex. One can not act even in the smallest way without his actions being charged with meaning. [2]

Twentieth-century man, perhaps more than any other, is necessarily

---

[1] Gabriel Celaya, *Poesía Urgente* (Buenos Aires: Editorial Losada, 1960), Introduction, p. 8.

[2] Somos ya tan, tan viejos que en vano procuramos hacer gestos sencillos, crear musica fácil. Cualquier cosa que hagamos se carga de sentido. (Gabriel Celaya, *Poesía urgente*, p. 29).

subjected to constant anguish if he is to take himself seriously.

> Te escuchas a ti mismo creyendo que preguntas.
> Eres un Europeo fatalmente enredado
> en las contra-respuestas de un yo tomado en serio.[3]

He finds himself caught in a psychological stalemate, he cannot move unless he is led out. His nature is that of a machine—a creature of habit that repeats the same errors because he is unaware and therefore unable to respond to the negative feedback he receives. Man is a goal-oriented animal that goes through action automatically after the goal has mentally been established.[4] It is the lack of perspective on this problem that keeps him from finding solutions. He cannot get to the problem without straightening out his mind, and he cannot straighten out his mind unless new goals replace the old ones. This calls for leaders who know man's nature first and foremost—why he is as he is and what causes history to repeat itself—disastrously, one might add. The transferral of this knowledge, consequently, becomes the responsibility of all who know it. The right kind of leaders must be bred in order to meet with understanding the actions and reactions that the present social systems have set in motion. Art and poetry in particular are tools to be used in the projected transformation. A deeper understanding has to be gained by more than one person.

The artist's task is no longer to describe the beauties of an unleashed imagination regardless of the splendor of his metaphor. An artist is first a man,[5] and as such he is responsible to himself and his fellow man. There is no time left for imagination. He must speak truth. He must discuss what happens in the street to you and me, that which concerns us all as fellow human beings. Man needs new goals, but first he needs to understand his own nature and where it will lead him if he never becomes aware of it. «Tuércele el cuello a lo innecesario,» says Celaya.

> Poesía para el pobre, poesía necesaria
> como el pan de cada día.[6]

---

[3] Gabriel Celaya, *Poesía*, p. 249.
[4] Gabriel Celaya, *Dos Cantatas.*
[5] Gabriel Celaya, «No basta ser poeta,» *Poesía urgente,* p. 52.
[6] *Ibid.*, p. 49.

Poetry is no longer to adorn; it is no longer a struggle for the beauty of rhyme; it is no longer to be a cultural luxury for neutrals. Man must take part. He must communicate what he knows to be truth to the utmost of his capacity; for it is only by super efforts that he can hope to sway the balance of power in favor of the organic. Poetry and art must be dynamic. They must be action directed through efforts to reach a higher level of thinking and understanding. A unified action on the part of all artists is necessary. One man can not make it alone; but if all became aware of their particular role as mediators, transmitters of knowledge, then there would be possibility. The possibility is small and the circumstances against it are giant, but to know and not to make an effort to do one's part is suicide. It would represent the death of hope.

The two poems that best express Celaya's attitude toward the position of poets in the world both past and present are «Vivir para ver» and «La poesía es una arma cargada de futuro.»[7] Celaya's main contention in these poems is that language and thought are subject to the law of change just as all things are. Therefore they must conform to this law. They must portray changing reality—they cannot be static. Moreover poetry must be taken personally and used as a key to further integrate the writer with life. A poet cannot remain neutral:

> Maldigo la poesía concebida como un lujo
> cultural por los neutrales
> que, lavándose las manos, se desentienden y evaden.

By taking on the faults and sufferings of others one becomes more himself.

> Hago mías las faltas. Siento en mí a cuantos sufren
> y canto respirando.
> Canto, y canto, y cantando más allá de mis penas
> personales, me ensancho.[8]

The purpose of the new poet is to motivate action, to lead men to the understanding that this is the only method of overcoming chaos. Poetry's first function is no longer beauty nor perfection; it must be an integral part of life—that which is necessary—action:

---

[7] Gabriel Celaya, *Poesía urgente*, pp. 49 and 50.
[8] *Ibid.*, p. 50.

Quisiera daros vida, provocar nuevos actos,
y calculo por eso con técnica, qué puedo.
Me siento un ingeniero del verso y un obrero
que trabaja con otros a España en sus aceros.

Tal es mi poesía: Poesía-herramienta
a la vez que latido de lo unánime y ciego.
Tal es, arma cargada de futuro expansivo
con que te apunto al pecho.

No es una poesía gota a gota pensada.
No es un bello producto. No es un fruto perfecto.
Es algo como el aire que todos respiramos
y es el canto que espacia cuanto dentro llevamos.

Son palabras que todos repetimos sintiendo
como nuestras, y vuelan. Son más que lo mentado.
Son lo más necesario: Lo que no tiene nombre.
Son gritos en el cielo, y en la tierra, son actos. [9]

He does not deny his debt to past poetry nor does he deny its beauty. Its purpose is what he questions.

Poca cosa me queda si resto lo que os debo,
ruiseñores maestros que os fuisteis por las ramas,
mas si canto, mi canto resulta diferente.
No quiero condenaros—¡ay, todo lo contrario!—.
Quisiera ser un hijo salvado y bautizado
mas pese a mí sucede que os niego en cada verso.
Lo que un día intentasteis sigue siendo un comienzo
que no puede seguirse. Somos otros, mordientes. [10]

Past poetry was not aware of needs of every day. It ignored and silenced those whose voices called to be heard in the name of humanity:

A veces me parece que os debo pedir cuentas,

---

[9] Gabriel Celaya, *Poesía urgente*, p. 50.
[10] *Ibid.*, p. 52.

no por mí, por aquellos que dejasteis sin habla
y estaban ya cargados de terrible evidencia
cuando dabais por buenas las técnicas, exactas
bellezas de unos versos que ahora nos avergüenzan
pues ya entonces lloraban los niños que os callabais,
maldecían los hombres que hoy siguen maldiciendo,
y vosotros, al margen, os lavabais las manos.

Debisteis dar palabras al mudo y al hambriento;
debisteis hablar alto por todos los que callan;
debisteis ser conciencia que crece cuando choca;
y tan sólo escribisteis unos versos neutrales.
No hablaría tan alto si no fuera sensible
a esas maquinaciones imparciales y bellas.
Lo que acuso en vosotros son mis propios pecados.
Faltasteis y he faltado. No basta ser poeta.[11]

It is not enough to be a poet. One must be concerned with real things rather than ideal essences. Celaya rebels against abstract concepts such as glory, honour, beauty, truth, goodness. They must be replaced by new concrete moral beliefs and new psychological doctrines:

«Nuestras cantares no pueden ser sin pecado un adorno.»[12] He literally denounces all past poets as liars and cheats lost in the realms of the imagination, unaware or unconcerned with the realities of man. They aid unconsciousness:

Contáis uno por uno los dientes a la luna
magnética y rabiosa de luz mortal e hiriente.
Inventáis el milagro con todo lo que cambia.
Jugáis al dominó con los huesos impares.
Levantáis un penacho casi fosforescente
de eléctrica inconsciencia, de foscos y alterados
insectos que crepitan en un claro de tierra
o libélulas leves que, liberadas, vuelan.[13]

[11]   Gabriel Celaya, *Poesía urgente*, p. 52.
[12]   *Ibid.*, p. 53.
[13]   Gabriel Celaya, *Poesía urgente*, p. 53.

Man is all the same; this is the basic point that past poets miss:

> Camaradas, quisiera deciros: No estáis solos.
> Quisiera que encontrarais en mis versos el eco
> del latido secreto que a todos nos sostiene,
> nos salva en el conjunto con una fe y mil rostros.
> Pueblo es Juancho Berridi, de profesión piloto,
> con todas sus virtudes y todos sus defectos.
> Pueblo es Ricardo Trecu, de oficio carpintero.
> Y pueblo yo con ellos que se creen traicionados. [14]

He describes his own poetry. The entire purpose and direction of his poetry can be seen in this very poem:

> Escuchad, camaradas, mis poemas íberos
> de hombre que, recorrido por vuestras mudas vidas,
> quisiera con sus versos lograr, no la belleza,
> sino la acción que pueden y deben los poetas
> promover con sus versos de conmovida urgencia.
> Recordad: No estáis solos. Recordad que si canto
> mal o bien canta dentro de mí, sin nombre, el pueblo,
> no abstracto, no eludido, ferozmente concreto. [15]

The overall picture of man's meaning and function in society is now so broad and complex that it is difficult to gain a proper perspective. Even for a conscious man it is difficult; for a machine of course it is out of the question. The solution Celaya suggests is through the various mediums of art, a unification of ideals and in particular the ideal of each man's responsibility in meeting the present day crisis. He calls on other artists and poets to aid in the transformation of society. He addresses his poems directly to them. Speaking to a sculptor, Andrés Basterra, also a Basque, he states:

> Tales son los oficios. Tales son las materias.
> Tal la forma de asalto del amor de la nuestra,
> la tuya, Andrés, la mía.
> Tal la oscura tarea que impone el ser un hombre.

---

[14] *Ibid.*, p. 54.
[15] *Ibid.*, p. 55.

Tal la humildad que siento. Tal el peso que acepto.
Tales los atrevidos esfuerzos contra un mundo
que quisiera seguirse sin pena y sin cambio,
pacífico y materno,
remotamente manso, durmiendo en su materia.
Tales, tercos, rebeldes, nosotros, con dos manos,
transformándolo, fieros, construimos un mundo
contra-naturaleza, gloriosamente humano.[16]

Celaya is very much like Jean Paul Sartre in his attitude toward the poet's function in society. The function they both have in mind is the transformation of society.

Past poetry will no longer suffice. Celaya's viewpoint is that the loss of time on the part of past poets is their irrevocable error. He describes this loss and its consequences in a poem entitled «Vivir para ver.» He begins his description with a very poetic yet precise definition of past poetry:

¡Distancias, espejismos!, hablemos despacito
del mundo que así cambia, dando vueltas, brillando
del pasado al futuro, del futuro a esa anchura
que se mira a sí misma sin decir lo que piensa,
propone, indefinida y absuelta, lo absoluto
con forma de muchacha simplemente bonita,
con versos simplemente felices que en la nada
rubrican la ironía con su líquido brillo.

Tal fue la poesía real y delirante
que ayer me fascinaba, sorbiéndome en sus giros:
Tobogán de caricias verso a verso cursadas
como una vuelta larga que resbala a ese trozo
de pueblo palpitante, voraz, real, violento
que hoy recojo caliente y el mar borra extendiendo.
Tal fue, nunca mordida, la evidencia increíble
que se rizaba al rizo con bucles de belleza.[17]

---

[16] Gabriel Celaya, *Poesía urgente*, pp. 20-21.
[17] Gabriel Celaya, *Poesía urgente*, p. 50.

Indeed he states it even more clearly for those perhaps not so attuned to metaphor:

Tales fuisteis vosotros, poetas vanguardistas,
rebeldes como un golpe de brisa entre las frondas,
levemente rebeldes, levemente reales,
apenas comprensibles hoy que vamos tan claro
cómo en falso eludisteis lo revolucionario
que os tocó y que puntuasteis jugando, no luchando,
y a título de bello burlando, no salvando
lo bárbaro y sagrado del impulso sin mancha.

He punctuates his disapproval with force, a force emphasized by the tragedy inherent in words like *irresponsable* and *ruinas*:

Bella fue la aventura. Bello fue vuestro impulso.
Bella la irresponsable radiación que exhibisteis.
Bellos, vuestros hallazgos. Bellos, los bellos versos
que quedan como ruinas de aquel viento de lejos
que no entendisteis, quiso ser un pueblo concreto
clamando en el desierto, llamando a vuestra puerta,
mientras, falsos rebeldes, creyéndoos combatientes,
arrojábais las bombas del lirismo absoluto.

This definition of past poetry and the poet's attitude toward it is followed immediately by a definition of «poesía pura, poesía directa,» Celaya's concept of ideal poetry and its necessary consequences:

¡Oh pura poesía luciente en lo lejano,
ave sobre-real de ojos bien calculados
y pupilas redondas de *atención delirante*![18]
¡Oh, construcción vibrátil de palabras exactas
e imágenes con brillo de explosiones de fiesta
que al estallar al cero perdían su sentido
y, al perder su sentido, desvelaban la magia
matemática y loca del verbo dicho y hecho!

---

[18]   Italics are mine.

Past poetry is a loss of time because it is not real, in the sense that it deals with illusions rather than realities. The real thing that it attempts to represent or re-interpret is at any rate so much better that silence would be the best thing a man could do in order to give the admittedly most beautiful all the time to show itself. However, since man in general, including poets, Celaya believes, are mechanical and cannot control their machines properly, they simply do not know when or how to be silent and when and how to speak. Indeed they do not even know for the most part that they are mechanical; they delude themselves to such a point that they have no desire to learn. Nevertheless poetry is one of the ways that enlightenment or knowledge can lead man out of his mechanical state. For a poet the writing of poetry is a way. One can see again that the paradox is a foundation of the entire life attitude of Gabriel Celaya the poet, and consequently of the whole of his poetry. He quotes as introduction to one part of his most important works, *Poesía urgente*: «Le voy a comunicar una sentencia *sagrada y misteriosa*: no hay nada superior al hombre.» «Lo demás es silencio . . . oh, oh, oh.» Man is superior in his capacity to gain understanding where originally he had none; he was created to be a self-evolving being that can gain consciousness and possess will.

The knowledge verified for Celaya through the writing of his poetry, and which he attempts to communicate is an understanding of the ultimate unity and interrelatedness of all things: feeling a part of instead of more or different or less or other than. A poet to Celaya is like other laborers, Pedro Echave Mazarredo, Juanita Andia, the «senora que lo que perdió en alegría lo ha ga-nado en dignidad,» or the old man who lost his strong sons over a war he did not even understand. The poet is a man whose talk is his way, his *linterna sorda*,[20] with which he views the face of all «fisiologia astral.»[21]

Luna: Gelatina
    visceral aprehendida
        en la red mis nervios
            fosforecentes.
Plexo en mis entrañas
    de agua nocturna,
        mas real que otras masas
            de sensación

---

[19]   Italics are mine.
[20]   Gabriel Celaya, *La linterna sorda* (Barcelona: El Bardo, 1964).
[21]   *Ibid.*, p. 9.

que nombramos: el brazo,
el hígado, el duodeno,
dragón del Secundario
domado en mis dentros.
Luna ciega: Medusa
de agua quemante y fuego
del aire suelto:
Luna activa y radiante.
De pronto, ya no sé
si estás dentro o fuera,
si eres órgano mío
o si yo pertenezco a tu sistema.
Reina de las tinieblas
más hondas:
Virgen terrible,
esposa del sol:
Mercúrio negro,
sal de luz violeta,
noche del día
de la violación.
Luna submarina
y tentacular,
magnético, me invade
tu arcaico horror.
Oceánica, tú, diosa
sin ojos. Y el sol.
El sol
único: El tirano!
Segundo plexo
de un resplandor:
Círculo y corona
de espadas llameantes:
Centro de un combate
que es en mí tan actual,
corazón, león feroz
devorando inmensidad,
palpito perdido,
vinagre esencial,
luz que a sí misma se muerde,

70

soledad.
Calor oculto
 del negro amor.
  Marea de Cieno.
   Turbio palpitar.
Nudo de serpientes
 que desenrosca el sol.
  Dolores: Sistema
   loco y circular,
que me hace el que soy,
 simple en apariencia,
  tan recién nacido.
   mojado de mar. [22]

Suffering requires strength, the strength to bear it and be happy «porque sí,» the only reason for happiness in Celaya's opinion.[23] Strength then makes suffering no longer suffering but something past it, a paradox: a whole made of the two parts, positive and negative—a new unity. It is this strength that Celaya sought: accepting what is as the truth and being silent since all else is false. One such manifestation of what is, or Truth, is the poet with his tool: his gift for language; his sensitivity to rhythm and timing, the proper hearing of a proper sound at the right moment in an attitude which brings an understanding to oneself, the poet, and perhaps indeed to others much the same as the poet. Poetry is a tool: «una arma cargada de futuro»:[24] an active force—dynamic poetry.

One is reminded of the literature of revolt and Camus' absurdist ethic. Man, whose goals and desires are thwarted by existence, revolts. He protests and leads to action as if things could change. He thus finds some sort of dignity. This type of dignity has courage at its heart. The courage to sacrifice with no hope for reward—only the hope to exist in the fullest, most meaningful manner. This type of conqueror is ultimately bound to Prometheus, who said:

---

[22] Gabriel Celaya, *Linterna Sorda* (Barcelona: El Bardo, 1964), p. 9.

[23] A la hora del aperitivo suelo estar contento por nada, por que sí, por todo. «Porque sí» es una buena razon: la única razón de la alegria. Si uno no está contento porque sí, no está vivo o no está sano. Gabriel Celaya, *Lo uno y lo otro* (Barcelona: Editorial Seix Barral, 1962).

[24] Gabriel Celaya, *Poesía urgente*, p. 49.

En face de la contradiction essentielle, je sortiens mon humaine contradiction. J'installe ma lucidité au milieu de ce qui la nie. J'exalte l'homme devant ce qui l'écrase et ma liberté, ma révolte et ma passion se rejoignent alors dans cette tension cette clairvoyance et cette répétition démesurée.[25]

In spite of his call to other artists in his proposed transformation, Celaya does not once forget the fundamental role and equality of the common man, what Spaniards term *pueblo*. Such men are the very backbone of life. In a poem entitled *A Sancho Panza* he states:

Sancho-claro, Sancho-recio,
Sancho que vistes las cosas como son y te callaste,
metiendo el hombro, tratando
de salvarnos del derrumbe con tu no lírico esfuerzo.

Hombre a secas, Sancho-patria, pueblo-pueblo,
pura verdad, fiel contraste
de los locos que te explotan para vivir del recuerdo,
¡ya ha llegado tu momento![26]

Celaya admires the simple ways of life and men close to nature and reality. He accuses passionately those who would rob them of the dignity and respect they merit:

Sancho-firme, Sancho-obrero,
ajustador, carpintero, labrador, electricista,
Sancho sin nombre y con manos de constructor y un oficio,
viejo y nuevo, vida al día.

Quiero darte la confianza que pretendieron robarte.
Quiero decirte quién eres.
Quiero mostrarte a ti mismo tal como tú fuiste siempre,
Sancho humilde, Sancho fuerte.

---

[25] Albert Camus, *Mythe de Sisyphe*, p. 120.
[26] Gabriel Celaya, *Poesía urgente*, p. 43.

En ti pongo mi esperanza
porque no fueron los hombres que se nombran los que hicieron
más acá de toda Historia—polvo y paja—nuestra patria,
sino tú como si nada.

Sancho-tierra, Sancho-santo, Sancho-pueblo,
tomo tu pulso constante,
miro tus ojos que brillan aún despúes de los desastres.
Tú eres quien es. ¡Adelante![27]

Celaya himself was most greatly influenced in life by the other artists he associated with or knew of only by their work. He actually lived in the same room where García Lorca and Salvador Dalí had lived. He admits the tremendous impression the lives of these two men had on him. Art really became foremost in his life in spite of his successful engineering career. It became the means for him to play his part in the transformation of society. It is to this goal and its accomplishment that he dedicates his life in word and action. He is a poet, and poetry becomes his tool, «una arma cargada de futuro.» He understands the enormousness of the scale of the change he proposes, but in the face of its vastness he does not cease to struggle. Celaya is a poet like Herrera with whom he admittedly identifies: «un hombre que sacrificó su vida a su obra, y que vivió para su obra y casi de su obra.»[28] With this in mind it is easy to see the reason his work is organic and reflects the same growth, depth and change of his life.

Celaya realizes that the revolution in society he speaks of cannot come simply through literature although the latter can help greatly. Even more important in this transformation is the access to the culture of social levels which until recently have lived in a completely natural state, but who now begin to speak out asking for another life.[29] For Celaya it is the manner in which the poet answers this call that determines his success as a poet and a man. Intelligent, conscious man acts in view of the fact that history repeats itself. Knowledge of a happening before it happens is a key to prevention if effort and organization is sufficiently strong. In other words, if the men in the system are strong enough to make it work.

---

[27] Gabriel Celaya, *Poesía urgente*, p. 44.

[28] Gabriel Celaya, *Exploración de la poesía* (Barcelona: Editorial Seix Barral S.A., 1964), p. 17.

[29] Gabriel Celaya, *Poesía urgente*, introduction, p. 8.

Celaya's poetry evolved in one definite direction in which the different stages represent both the surgical and healing aspects of his solution, as well as a diagnosis of man's principal problems and their manifestations. One can see the reaffirmation of Celaya's philosophy through his actions and life style. He believes that if all artists write and portray faithfully the truth of their experience, knowledge of esoteric doctrines can be maintained and understood on a more practical level. The concrete reality of Celaya's experience was that it was not play that led to success, but work, living as best you can, working as best you can and loving as best you can, putting maximum effort into things. The rules of religious leaders such as Christ and Buddha are the rules of life now at the moment; man is God, or if you will, conscious man is a supreme being. Man kills himself because he does not understand this. He forgets he is so much and becomes negative, which leads to hate of oneself and others.[30] These rules are man's rules and he must honor them. Man must respect himself, and in his heart he understands or feels what is right. If he does not follow it, then he cannot be at ease. A man must either do a thing or not, but he can not deceive himself. «Thou shalt not kill» does not refer only to other people, but to everyone. It is a cosmic law; thus, those who do not live by such laws suffer from them.

It is Celaya's belief that the supreme being is a pattern toward which man must struggle. Man can become a supreme being, but he is not born that way; his evolution lies in his own hands.[31] Such evolution can be gained with effort if circumstances permit. To be supreme at anything requires great effort. That is the way of life. If supremacy were easily gained, its value would be less—it is a question of degree. Consciousness cannot be given; by its very nature it must be earned. One cannot take any man off the street and make him a general. He would not know what to do. Things must be earned so they can be properly controlled. The masses, however, are lazy. Inertia is the trademark of unconscious man. He does not want to work so he plays games and uses his genius for the wrong purpose. Consequently he becomes more and more mechanical, completely unaware of the reality going on all around him. Worse than lazy—he is asleep and does not hear the onrush of the tide. It is the poet's place, the artist's place—man's place—to aid now in the best way he can. He must aid himself and those around him as far as he can; although man's nature is complex and difficult or impossible to understand completely, inertia we do understand and must fight. This is one of the prin-

---

30 Gabriel Celaya, *Dos cantatas*, passim.
31 *Ibid.*

ciples that Celaya calls on artists to illustrate in *Poesía urgente*. There are to be new rules. One must work to understand—work—at what one can do best. Artists must unite in an effort to put an end to the holocaust of war and destruction. They must teach the value of simplicity and that one must work in his own garden as Voltaire attempted to teach two centuries earlier.

V
Style

Celaya's poetry provides one of the clearest and most successful illustrations of the modern revolt in poetry which began in Spain around 1946. The essence of this revolution can be found in the shift in the poet's attitude toward himself and his fellow artists as well as their function and meaning in life and society. For the revolutionary poet of this period (particularly in Spain) responsibility and truth became key notes. [1] It was Celaya's belief that no man, if he is really alive and aware, has the right to refuse to do his share in the struggle against the evident world chaos and disorder because to refuse is to admit hopelessness and despair. Verse forms could no longer be cultivated for their own sake. Style and theme were both subordinated to aim and purpose—or at least congruous with it. It is precisely this long range aim and this attitude of responsibility which Celaya never loses sight of that is the cause of the excellent unification found in his work. Style becomes theme and theme, style: an integrated tool structured by the poet to work for the transformation of society. The nearer goal in the path of the long range aim of this social transformation is to bring individual man to the possibility of change by means of acquiring a higher level of consciousness. Celaya's poetry is extraordinary in that it does not simply provide knowledge of an intellectual sort but a system of practical experiences which point to a method of change in being. This system is seen in its most explicit form in the long poem entitled «Dos cantatas.» Celaya completely rejects traditional verse forms and rhyme

---

[1]   Information taken from tape sent by Celaya.

schemes because they were seemingly unaware of the necessary aim of social revolution required of art and poetry. The value of a poem must be judged in view of whether or not it leads in the direction of that aim. Poetry which does not, is not necessary and therefore mechanical. The new creed of the Generation of '46 to which Celaya states he belongs, was the valuelessness of all that is unnecessary. «Tuércele el cuello a lo innecesario,» shouts Celaya. [2]

Celaya's poetry evolved into a complex and inclusive approach in which the symbol, his principal technique, defines and modifies with one stroke the multifold connotations of ordinary words. Modern living is no longer simple —nothing is simple any longer. Everything—idea and word—is permeated with meaning. Celaya realizes this and in view of his creed of «lo necesario» he does not give the reader an abstraction in the guise of experience. He is consistently faithful to the complexity and detail of experience.

What Celaya endeavors and achieves by this method is a revelation of the subtle relationships between events and phenomena which have otherwise seemed separate—a new dimension of knowledge. He tries through poetry to put into practice his ideas on the relationships between man's language and man's thinking; how the latter is actually caused by the former in a very mechanistic, unromantic way; and that only through purification of language can come purification of thought. It is from this point of view that we must approach the problem of style and technique in Celaya's poetry.

Celaya's style of writing can be classified into three basic approaches which varied according to circumstance and the stage of evolution of the poet's view of life. The approach which made its appearance with his first volume of verse published in 1934 had an undeniably mystic orientation in regard to subject matter as well as technique. The second approach, which did not appear until ten years later, is drastically different. It is a type of prose poetry whose principal themes are political, social and cultural similarly structured on the paradoxical meanings of language due to the various levels of understanding and to intense diversity and complication of the various patterns after the original, modified by time and the historical changes it has brought. The third and latest approach is the dramatic form which reminds one very much of García Lorca and Lope de Vega. The poems of this latter period are all extremely long, dramatically structured poems in which all the characters assume a symbolic role often representative of the various levels of consciousness, which is their principal theme. The poetry here is direct state-

---

[2] Gabriel Celaya, *Poesía urgente* (Buenos Aires: Editorial Losada, 1960), p. 53.

ment, but the imagery is startlingly vivid.

In spite of the fact that each of these styles has an exceedingly different tone and feeling, the dominant themes, already outlined in detail, are consistently unified because Celaya's poetry is developed within a coordinated system to such an extent that whatever type work he produces is simply a variation, or a microscopic vision of a portion or angle of the whole.

The first phase of Celaya's style, which was cut short by the outbreak of civil war, can be described most accurately as modern mystic. As already mentioned, the influence of oriental mysticism is more evident than Christian mysticism. The title of the author's first volume of verse and the one which won him the coveted *Prémio Béquer Centenario* is *Soledad cerrada* and begins its title page with a quotation from the Hindu mystic writings, the Upanishad-Brihadayanka:

«en el origen nada existía sino Atman.
miró en torno a sí y solo se
vió a sí mismo.
entonces deseó un segundo ser.»[3]

This second being is a portion of oneself in reality and from the very first instance the theme of enlightenment and at the same time man's bitter isolation and alienation manifest themselves. The first poem of the series reveals these themes. It is called «Quien me habita» and the subtitle is a quotation from Rimbaud, «Car je est un autre.» In Chapter III there was a more comprehensive discussion of the poetic technique as well as a more detailed analysis of theme. The second phase of Celaya's style, exemplified by such works as *Tranquilamente hablando* and «Lo demás es silencio,» came to light between 1946 and 1951 and formed an important part of the poetry of revolt called *Poesía social*.

The poems written in this period differ from one another considerably in length and complexity. However on the whole they can be divided into two main categories: the shorter, somewhat more personally oriented poems and the later extremely long dramatic poems. The latter most successfully portray the poet's understanding of the nature of politics and its relationship to

---

[3] Gabriel Celaya, *Poesía* (1934-61) (Madrid: Ediciones Giner, 1962), title page.

individual man. The following is a representative example of the shorter poem:

Cuéntame cómo vives;
dime sencillamente cómo pasan tus días,
tus lentísimos odios, tus pólvoras alegres
y las confusas olas que te llevan perdido
en la cambiante espuma de un blancor imprevisto.

Cuéntme cómo vives.
Ven a mí, cara a cara;
dime tus mentiras (las mías son peores),
tus resentimientos (yo también los padezco),
y ese estúpido orgullo (puedo comprenderte).

Cuéntame cómo mueres.
Nada tuyo es secreto:
La náusea del vacío (o el placer, es lo mismo);
la locura imprevista de algún instante vivo;
la esperanza que ahonda tercamente el vacio.

Cuéntame cómo mueres.
cómo renuncias—sabio—,
cómo—frívolo—brillas de puro fugitivo,
cómo acabas en nada
y me enseñas, es claro, a quedarme tranquilo [4]

One can see here Celaya's narrative, almost prose-like style. Although there is a measured rhythm, there is no attempt at rhyme with the possible exception of irregular assonance in i-o. There are four five-line strophes. The approach is direct and simple, in perfect tune with the theme which is explicit and easily understood.

The second category, the long, dramatic poems, although equally direct and written in almost prose form, is much more complex and difficult to understand. The length of course is one important factor. «Lo demás es silencio,» one of the poems of this category and period, is 78 pages long. More important, however, as far as complication and difficulty of understanding is

---

[4]   Gabriel Celaya, *Poesía* (1934-61), p. 189.

concerned, is the poet's structured use of the symbol in these long poems. This technique is one of the distinguishing features of Celaya's poetry. He uses it to unify the main works of his entire poetic output. The characters are symbols in the dramatic poems which represent philosophical points of view that are supposedly the basis of certain political and social realities of twentieth century man. In later poetry they represent mythical points of view. In «Lo demás es silencio» (1951), a work Celaya considers one of his most important, the protagonist, called «protagonista,» is symbolic of the purely existential view of life. The messenger, called «el mensajero,» symbolizes Marxism, and the choir «coro» is the Spanish people—«el pueblo.» The poem develops dramatically in the dialectic fashion, and offers no ostensible solution. The conflict or seemingly contradictory and insolvable positions are simply presented.

The overall structure of the symbols, however, is very complex and functions as an implicit tie or interrelationship between one level of existence or consciousness and another. The primary underlying idea or philosophic attitude at the base of this structure is the notion that all action or happenings are composed of three forces: First force, second force, and third force, or active, passive, and neutralizing. All three of these forces must be present for the sequence of reactions to occur. All of the long dramatic poems have these three basic forces in the key positions. Each poem has two seemingly contradictory points of view and action, and a third which serves as a buffer or a neutralizing agent. All concrete details of the principle are actually variations of the pattern which is usually the idea of the law of three forces: force, resistance, and neutralizing agent. The «protagonista,» «mensajero,» and «coro» in «Lo demás es silencio» are an example. *Ingeniero, Mono,* and *Ezbá* in *Dos cantatas* are another.

The third period of Celaya's style is characterized by long dramatic poems which represent the best of his latest verse and exhibit a perfection of the various poetic techniques already analyzed. The best and most representative volume of this period is called *Dos cantatas.* This volume contains two long poems, «El derecho y el revés» and «Cantata en Aleixandre,» one of which has already been analyzed in detail. The level of expression of the basic themes in this type of poetry is again different from the other two categories or approaches already discussed. The dominant themes are no longer presented from the point of view of social myth, or politics of society, but rather from a point of view of the spiritual aspects of man, i.e., what he was created capable of attaining as compared with what he has actually attained up to the present. This development was examined in detail in Chapter II.

Perhaps the most striking aspect of the poetry of this period as well as his entire poetic production is the artist's extraordinarily effective handling of tone. Tone is not an attitude adopted by the poet for its own sake but is a technique or a tool used by the poet for a specific effect. In the long dramatic works each poem is a story into which the anguish of the human predicament is projected. The commentary on this predicament is not stated as a conclusion but is rather diffused throughout the story creating step by step the tone and feeling of the poem. In this manner the tone becomes so intimately and vitally a part of the theme and meaning of the total poem that it does Celaya an injustice to quote fragments of his poetry. In the following quotation although the language is almost prosaic, it has been elevated poetically by means of tone and profundity of feeling emotionally the truth of a thing. The theme relates so directly to the tone that the one simply does not exist without the other. Celaya creates the poem's tone deliberately, setting the scene, so to speak, for the revelation of his beliefs in the meaning and nature of existence. He speaks his own truth just as he feels it from his own personal point of view. He is isolated:

> Desde el asteroide Ge-Celaya-Cincuenta,
> con cielo despejado y, en mi centro, un bostezo,
> hoy veintitrés de junio, tan sin pena ni gloria,
> mientras con viento fresco me lleva el Nor-Nordeste,
> te saludo, Miguel, por si acaso aún existes.[5]

His isolation is indicated by the word *asteroide*. He is so isolated he compares himself to a piece of material in space by its very nature doomed to solitude. The monotony and melancholy of this situation are heightened by the use of rhythm; it is almost motionless. Added to his isolation is the factor of his own lack of control as far as destiny or personal direction is concerned. He is *carried* by the north-northeast with the wind. The fellow poet he greets, he greets in case he still exists, intimating by tone that the certainty of life and knowledge is at a minimum. There is, however, no romantic emotional outpouring of despair. The statement is simple and direct, made from the realistic point of view of man isolated and remote. Thus the tone is established. It is strange—not completely celestial and yet not completely earthly.

The speaker, who is Celaya himself, thus acts «as though» Miguel Laboreta (a pseudonym for the exiled poet Miguel Hernández to whom the poem

---

[5] Gabriel Celaya, *Poesía urgente*, pp. 26-27.

is directed) is alive although it has already been stated that one cannot be sure. He speaks the poem to his peer, telling him that the latest news is sad: «Se casan nuestras adolecentes con notorios; se ríen en mis barbas los hombres de negocios; la brisa sólo es brisa—no un ángel extraviado—: y Dios, allá en su cielo, sigue siendo un Dios mudo.»[6] The tone becomes more and more complex and subtle. The dominant themes are repeated, but they are set in a new light so to speak. Tone and emphasis are changed by changing points of view or perspective. The theme of man's lack of consciousness is present for example; but the tone or feeling is personal. In this poem man's lack of consciousness and its meaning and effect are related personally and directly to Celaya himself first and then to other men with whom he attempts to relate himself. It makes him personally afraid to see dead men walk:

> Da miedo ver las gentes que pasan por las calles.
> Si uno les preguntara su nombre no sabrían
> qué contestar en serio, qué decir limpiamente.
> Yo les dejo que pasen bajando la cabeza.
> No quiero ver. Me asusta que los muertos caminen.
>
> Más vale estar callado. No vaya a ser que al ruido
> de «¿qué tal su familia? La mía, muy bien, gracias»,
> algunos se den cuenta de que estaban ya muertos,
> que no tienen sentido, ni un yo con nombre fijo,
> y entonces se desplomen odiándose a sí mismos.[7]

He strengthens the unity and co-ordination of the poem by directly addressing the poet to whom it is written: «Quizas Miguel debiera callar tanta gloria excesiva, tanto día barato.»[8]

One can see further complication of the tone by an exploration of the multiple relationships within the poem's context. The speaker relates himself to the poet addressed:

> mas me asustan un poco tus tremendas preguntas:
> «¿De dónde diablos vengo?» y «¿qué hago aquí pensando?»

6 Gabriel Celaya, *Poesía urgente*, p. 27.
7 *Ibid.*
8 *Ibid.*

Comprende. Éstas son cosas que no deben decirse.[9]

Then the speaker reveals his personal attitude toward Miguel Laboreta:

> Ya sé que hablas en serio como un mágico niño,
> como un hombre excesivo, como un Dios en proyecto.
> Ya sé que tus bostezos de tarde de domingo
> desfondan cero a cero tus últimas defensas,
> te abren los trascendentes e irónicos abismos.[10]

The dramatic element plays an important role in Celaya's handling of tone. In the above poem which is representative of this period, the early lines are dedicated to setting the scene, or the tying of the knot. Then comes the climax and finally the denouement. The climax of the poem under analysis is easily recognized. It is distinguished by a much more emotional as opposed to intellectual approach. Theory and idea give way to feeling—to like and dislike—to a turbulent shout in praise of the simplicity and beauty of existence:

> Me gustas cuando dices «gracias» a cualquier cosa.
> Gracias al tranviario que te ha dado un billete,
> gracias a tu bobita, y a un amigo—un Don Nadie—.
> que ocupa un lugar cierto como una nube-instante.
> Me gustas si te noto puntualmente contento.
>
> Dejemos las preguntas de ayer para mañana.
> Gocemos del presente: Ser ahora mismo un hombre.
> ¡Qué bello es ese tilo dorado que contemplo!
> ¿Bonito? ¡Sí! Bonito. Simplemente bonito
> como el mundo evidente cuando miro tranquilo.[11]

The height of the climax occurs about two-thirds of the way through the poem. It is strong, decidedly a sample of Celaya's most lyric verse:

---

[9]   Gabriel Celaya, *Poesía urgente*, p. 27.
[10] *Ibid.*, p. 28.
[11] Gabriel Celaya, *Poesía urgente*, p. 29.

Sorbo tu poesía, Miguel, como un Martini,
un Paul Eluard, un giro que no sé adónde lleva
y en su hora pura es sólo como un latido sordo
de vena violeta de plata corrosiva
en una ganga amorfa que duerme, pesa, duerme.

Me encantas. Me fastidias. Me drogas. Me vulneras.
Son las cóleras dulces del aire sin secretos
y es la mujer silvestre que ahora toco y no veo.
Son las llamas contrarias de un día violento,
las ideas que giran sobre un supuesto centro.

Ser único, ser Dios, así como si nada.
Ser, pese a lo imperfecto, poeta inevitable.
Ser un hombre en el aire que no pesa ni piensa,
que burla porque sufre, que llora porque existe,
que, sin culpa, se sabe mortal e inigualable.[12]

The denouement ensues abruptly by introducing again the personal tone:
«Pero vuelvo a decirte, Miguel.» The downward or settling tone of the poem
continues like a wake after the ship of tragedy. The speaker, Celaya, states
again his own exceedingly personal reality:

No explico. No discuto. No intento convencerte.
No me mido con otros. No lucho contra nadie.
No quiero ser distinto—ser más, ser, ser matando—.
No insisto. Pongo sólo delante de tus ojos
mis restos de alegría salvados del desastre.

Tantas complicaciones, tanta belleza fútil,
tantas delicadezas de un Don Yo vulnerable,
tanta hambre sin sentido que a veces se agiganta
y cree que si los otros se achican, Don Yo crece,
me invitan a ser pobre, banal, mudo, cualquiera.

Por lo demás, si quieres saber cómo me arreglo,
teniendo siempre en cuenta que encima del tejado

---

[12]   *Ibid.*, p. 31.

maúllan a la luna metafísica y gato,
que debemos torcerle el cuello a lo excesivo,
te contaré las horas que aun puedo llamar vida.[13]

The overwhelming truth of his statement and its application to all of mankind is illustrated explicitly in concrete detail by Celaya's own personal example which he has had the courage, intelligence and responsibility as a man and a poet of the twentieth century to communicate to his fellow man. The tone and idea are inseparable.

Man is no more and no less than a man. He has the magnificent gift of life, yet he must die and he knows it. Life in reality is a paradox, a contradiction in which one must live from dying—live from dedicating oneself and exhausting one's energy. Celaya describes the contradiction as it exists within him as a man and a poet: the style is prosaic, the tone realistic.

La sed con que he bebido cerveza esta mañana,
la muchacha que anoche besé rendidamente
con ansia que crecía, y hoy besaré igualmente,
y estar en la terraza fumando hora tras hora
resumen sin más cuentos mi vida de existente.

Si te contara todo, si fuera eso posible,
si abriera en estos versos un solo instante pleno,
si vieras cuánto exaltan los gozos materiales,
cuánta vida contienen los hechos mas sencillos,
Miguel, disfrutarías de ser hombre finito.

No luches. No propagues. Contente en tu momento.
Deja las extensiones a Dios que sabe y calla.
Dimite de tu carga de orangután celeste.
No charles más. No grites. No hagas versos extraños.
No imites al Ausente. Recuerda: Eres un hombre.

Vestirse, alimentarse, ganar el pan, morirse,
no son cosas vulgares aunque tú así lo dices.
Ver a las pobres gentes sonámbulas que pasan

---

[13] Gabriel Celaya, *Poesía urgente*, p. 31.

es olvidarse un poco de que uno es pobre gente,
creer que porque mira de lejos es divino.

Mas tú también te mueres. Mas yo también me muero.
Somos seres cualquiera y hombres extraordinarios
capaces de entregarse por una idea, un beso,
un pájaro, un absurdo, un mero «eso es posible»,
unos preliminares de vida en subjuntivo.

Todo esto forma parte del ser mortal que somos.
Vivimos de morirnos. Vivimos de entregarnos.
Vivimos de ser otros, cambiando, entusiasmados.
Somos las disponibles conciencias descentradas,
perdidas, extasiadas en todo lo que existe.[14]

    The conclusion of the poem is unique in that it is Celaya's own analysis of the poem's style as well as a comparison of other poets including Miguel Laboreta. Commentary on the latter is composed of a summarized statement of Celaya's own principal poetic theme: *las enigmas contrarias*:

No sé por qué te escribo. No sé muy bien qué digo.
Noto cómo me invade lo oceánico y no acabo.
Cada palabra escrita me compromete un tanto
por ciento de las aves, hermosas si volando,
suciamente expirantes si las guardo en un puño.

Si en esta carta larga con más viento que vela
no he dicho lo contrario de aquello que he intentado,
si no pasa por ella mi más que pensamiento,
Miguel, soporta el fardo de un nuevo amigo inútil,
soporta mis fracasos de vuelos vueltos versos.

Adiós, Nerón Jiménez, de dientes inclementes.
Adiós, Valdemar triste, tan bello entre las nubes,
que crecen cuando, lenta, la tarde todo olvida.
Adiós, Miguel, amigo, pequeño, raro, hermano.

---

[14]   Gabriel Celaya, *Poesía urgente*, p. 32.

Adiós a los enigmas contrarios que tú encierras.[15]

Another technique Celaya uses to create tone, and one which at the same time unites the theme of his poetry to his style is the anaphora. He repeats key words and sounds in order to make a particular idea more profound or complex. An excellent example of this particular use of the anaphora is seen in a poem entitled «A Blas de Otero.» His preoccupation with the nature of existence is implicit in the repetition of words like *soy*:

Soy creciente; me muero. Soy materia: palpito
Soy un dolor antiguo como el mundo que aún dura
. . . .
Soy coral, soy muchacha, soy sombra y aire nuevo,
Soy el tordo en la zarza, soy la luz en el trino
Soy estrella, soy tigre, soy niño y soy diamante.

Soy un hombre perdido,
Soy mortal, soy cualquiera.[16]

Another word repeated frequently which also reveals his principal thematic concerns is *nada*:

Yo, abrazado a mi nada:
—nada mía querida

. . . .
¿Nacerás nada mía?
densísimo silencio?

. . . .
¿Donde estás, nada mía?

. . . .
Unos y otros, todos nada...[17]

A technique the poet uses with equal consistency in the creation of tone, evident in this same poem, is the question. His constant use of the question

---

[15] Gabriel Celaya, *Poesía*, p. 218.
[16] *Ibid.*, p. 243.
[17] Gabriel Celaya, *Poesía*, pp. 91-92.

reinforces his attitude of concern and his desire to find solutions for man's predicament, as well as meaning in his own existence. It at times indicates uncertainty, searching and disorientation:

¿Porqué? ¿Para qué? ¿Hasta cuándo?[18]
¿Quién es quien es? ¿Quién vive? ¿Quién de verdad se muestra?
. . . .
Mas ¿Quién soy yo? ¿Quién soy? Sólo un fantasma.[19]

The mere fact of existence and society is completely overwhelming to him:

¿Que hago aquí, como puedo pedir que me
consientan disfrutar de ese lujo
que es tener un servicio de taxis y unos guardias
que le dicen a uno por donde se va a casa?[20]

Along with the frequent use of the question there is an abundant use of exclamations (epiphonema) which furthers the creation of tone. This device is not always used to indicate felicity as one might expect, however, although this is sometimes the case; more often it is simply used to add force and a dynamic feeling to the verse:

¡Pobre de mí! ¡Pobres de los que, pobres
lloramos los sudores,
creyéndonos divinos, gota a gota acabando
en esa cristalina verdad que transparenta
lo mucho que debemos, lo poco que valemos,
la nada de los nombres![21]

In much of Celaya's poetry one finds a profound note of melancholy which stems from his preoccupation with man's present position. This melancholy is portrayed not only through theme but also through such poetic techniques as anaphora, alliteration and rhythm. Note the slow monotonous rhythm combined with anaphora and alliteration in the following poem:

---

[18]   *Ibid.*, p. 162.
[19]   *Ibid.*, p. 276.
[20]   *Ibid.*
[21]   Gabriel Celaya, *Poesía*, p. 271.

¡Qué extraño es verme aquí sentado,
y cerrar los ojos, y abrirlos, y mirar
y oír como una lejana catarata que la vida se derrumba,
y cerrar los ojos, y abrirlos, y mirar![22]

The poem is almost static. The tone is modified by rhythm which places emphasis at certain points, thus reinforcing and conditioning the underlying thought.

Another poetic technique with which Celaya becomes extraordinarily accomplished and which enables him to unite his theme and technique is the symbol. The seeds of this remarkable talent are found in this early mystic verse. Symbol can be defined as a single word or a few short words which embody several ideas at once. For a complete understanding of each particular symbol all the ideas plus the order in which they occur or the order of emphasis must be grasped. What Celaya attempts with the use of the symbol is a new type of thinking in terms of non-space-time dimension. Poetry to Celaya means density of meaning, i.e., the depth to which words are charged with meaning. Cleanth Brooks defines symbolist poets in the following manner:

> The symbolist poet refuses to sacrifice the subtlety and complexity of his total vision of reality. Such a poetry will undoubtedly result in a limitation of the audience, but the limitation will be an unfortunate necessity conditioned by the nature of the poetry.[23]

The symbolist can achieve a depth of emotional and oftentimes spiritual feeling without violating the realistic detail in the situation. The concrete details of the experience are related firmly and realistically by these poems but further metaphorical extension is undeniably suggested.

Indeed the key to the use of the symbol in Celaya's poetry is that in spite of the use of this poetic figure his art reveals the concrete reality of what a person actually experiences, rather than an abstract idea or statement. The reader is symbolically presented the concrete and dramatic aspect of experience in the existential pattern. Celaya believed that abstract truths like those of Marxism and democracy have led man too far from reality, i.e., his

---

[22] *Ibid.*, p. 13.
[23] Cleanth Brooks, *Modern Poetry and the Tradition* (Chapel Hill: The University of North Carolina Press, 1939), p. 59.

own personal reality. Abstracts relate to divine things; concrete detail relates to man. These are two distinct levels and their interrelationships must be grasped to have true understanding.

Note the almost personal tone of the following poem of his mystic period entitled «Presencia.» One is reminded of San Juan de la Cruz' «Noche obscura del alma.» Here «Luna» is the principal symbol, a presage, a dead adolescent girl floating in a water of distant music. The moon although an external symbol is seen inwardly:

¡Oh noches, cuando absorto, hundiéndome en mí mismo,
veía en el cristal de mi clausura helada
un presagio, la luna, la adolescente muerta
flotando en un agua de músicas lejanas!

¡Oh noches, cuando inmóvil, con los ojos en blanco,
descendí a lo más hondo de mi inerte silencio![24]

The moon is symbolic of death:

La muerte se acercaba con un lirio en la mano,
suelta su cabellera de luz fría y delgada,
se inclinaba sobre mí para besarme,
murmuraba a mi oído sus secretos.[25]

But the death was an inward one intimately bound with the mystery of oneself, existence, and consciousness:

Eran las delicias y también los peligros
escondidos en las simas de uno mismo:
Virgen crucificada en mis brazos abiertos!,
tan íntima que tan solo tu presencia ya me duele.[26]

Note the confusion between the perceptions of the different senses. «Comme de longs èchos qui de loin se confondent . . . . . . Les parfums, les couleurs et les sons se repòndent,» Baudelaire stated in his poem «Correspondance.»

---

[24] Gabriel Celaya, *Poesía* (1934-61), p. 21.
[25] *Ibid.*
[26] Gabriel Celaya, *Poesía* (1934-61), p. 21.

Celaya describes «luz fría y delgada» and the «lenta destrucción de la tarde reflejada en los ojos dorados del suicida.» The moon symbol continues its structure of complexity. He becomes the night of the moon's body:

Bajaba a tus abismos, me entregaba a tus fiebres,
buscándote, virgen, en este aislamiento;
mi cerrada clausura de amianto y de vidrio
era tu madreperla, la noche de tu cuerpo.[27]

The moon is described in detail, white, cold, lover, enemy, vice, martyrdom, blind, suffering, living by being what is silenced:

Virgen blanca y helada, a ti me condenaba,
mi amante, mi enemiga, mi vicio, mi martirio.

Te veía ciega, delirando en mi noche,
sufriendo y viviendo de ser lo que se calla;[28]

The symbol of the moon also connotes man's ultimate nature and origin, the pattern of not knowing and awe in the face of the miracle and anguish of life:

eras un estremecimiento de desnudez y origen:
en mi carne de sombra, calofrío de plata.
Te esperaba, esperaba tu tránsito de nieve,
la anunciación del alba de tu cuerpo desnudo,
la alegría naciendo a flor de espuma y beso,
la muerte, fiel reposo de mi inquietud en ti.

¡Amor!, yo te miraba con rubor de silencio,
cerraba los ojos, te daba sed mi vida,
virgen casi naciendo, hablándome casi,
en la atmósfera helada de ausencia enrarecida.[29]

The final aspect of the moon symbol is paradoxical. She is addressed as the «Celeste Immaculada de mis soledades,» a solitude so real and profound that

---

[27] *Ibid.*, p. 22.
[28] *Ibid.*
[29] Gabriel Celaya, *Poesía* (1934-61), pp. 22-23.

it was almost alive:

> ¡qué viva te sentía dentro de mí mismo!
> Ya casi te veía, lucífaga, profounda,
> tendida bajo el árbol de los escalofríos.[30]

Thus symbols become chains or paths of connections in Celaya's poetry which hold true not only in the context of one particular poem but in his entire poetic output. In this manner he attempts to delve below the dry isolated word exteriors to the similarities between seemingly unrelated ideas.

Metaphysical or mystic and symbolic poetry are related in the subtlety of their descriptions of feelings. In 1964, almost thirty years later in a poem entitled «Fisiología,» the moon is still referred to with the same symbolic connotations:

> Luna ciega: Medusa
> de agua quemante y fuego
> del aire suelto:
> Luna activa y radiante.

> De pronto, ya no sé
> si estás dentro o fuera,
> si eres órgano mío
> o si yo pertenezco a tu sistema.

> Reina de las tinieblas
> más hondas:
> Virgen terrible,
> esposa del sol:[31]

Here the mystic tone is absent however. The style is the second, more prosaic approach, characteristic of the poetry of these years. The statement is more direct, but the symbolism is unaltered. Better said, it is basically the same with thirty years of complication. The symbol of the Sun now complicates and clarifies the moon symbol. Speaking to the moon the poet says:

---

[30] *Ibid.*, p. 23.
[31] Gabriel Celaya, *Linterna Sorda* (Barcelona: El Bardo, 1964), p. 9.

Luna submarina
    y tentacular,
        magnética, me invade
            tu arcaico horror.

Oceánica, tú, diosa
    sin ojos. Y el sol.
        El sol
            único: El tirano![32]

The moon and the sun are two plexus within the poet which form the center of an internal combat between the day forces or enlightenment: *Sol*, and the night forces or mechanicalness: *Luna*.

Segundo plexo
    de un resplandor:
        Círculo y corona
            de espadas llameantes:

Centro de un combate
    que es en mi tan actual,
        corazón, león feroz
            devorando inmensidad,[33]

The system is a synthesis of opposites generating one from another into existence.

First force: sol

    pálpito perdido,
        vinagre esencial,
            luz que a sí misma se muerde,
                soledad.

Second force: luna

---

[32] Gabriel Celaya, *Poesía*, pp. 9-10.
[33] Gabriel Celaya, *Poesía*, p. 10.

Calor oculto
   del negro amor.
      Marea de Cieno
         Turbio palpitar.[34]

First force or *luna* is a knot of serpents which the second force, sun, en-
twines, a mad circular system which generates pain, yet, paradoxically
enough, life:

   Nudo de serpientes
      que desenrosca el sol.
      Dolores: Sistema
         loco y circular,

   que me hace el que soy,
      simple en apariencia,
         tan recién nacido,
            mojado de mar.[35]

Celaya's basic method which serves as a scaffolding for this type of symbolism can be illustrated by a careful examination of the structure of his best
poetry. The core of all his poetry with only a few exceptions is structured on a
paradox: a major contrast between two types of life and two types of death.
Life and death as ordinary man knows them and the particular meaning of
life and death from the point of view of gaining enlightenment, rebirth or consciousness. This paradoxical structure is particularly evident in the mystic
period but still stridently recognizable in his most recent poems. The structure
of his poetry is multi-dimensional due to the clumsy instruments of mind and
language he must use in his investigation of very subtle matters and subtle
problems.

One can see from only a glimpse of the verse representative of the three
main classifications of Celaya's work (mystic, prosaic and dramatic) that the
principal themes and the main objectives are never lost. By a truly remarkable use of the symbol he deepens the significance of his themes and creates
a strong unity within his entire poetic production. He renders the use of the
symbol more effective by careful attention to tone, which he creates by the

---

[34] *Ibid.*
[35] *Ibid.*

use of anaphora, alliteration and rhythm. The overall effect of his verse is consequently extraordinary and his theme well communicated.

Conclusion

The major theme in Celaya's poetry is the nature of man and its reflection in the moral, intellectual and political climate of the world of our time. The poet questions and explores both the traditional and future values of mankind, their causes and their effects. What meaning is there in life? What is man's place and significance in the great scheme of things, or indeed the small? The poet concerns himself principally throughout his work with the possibility of man's evolution and development which at this stage must be psychological. Celaya believes most ordinary men are presently asleep or unconscious and completely unaware of the great powers within their reach. Indeed they are unaware of most things—even the reality in which they live and die. Celaya studies the methods needed for man to extricate himself from this stalemate and concludes that super efforts will have to be made; only by effort can one gain understanding.

The theme of the paradox which actually serves as a substructure for all his poetry is the axis on which these ideas concerning man's possibility of consciousness turn. Man is dead (unconscious) and yet he can live by ceasing to be what he presently is. He must die to live (vivir rompiéndose). The idea of perpetual change is the keynote of these ideas (existential becoming):

> Y aceptadlo sabiendo que también lo que hoy clama
> parecerá mañana traición. Por eso canto:
> ¡Distancias, espejismos! hablemos despacito
> del mundo que así cambia, dando vueltas, brillando. [1]

---

[1] Gabriel Celaya, *Poesía urgente* (Buenos Aires: Editorial Losada, S.A., 1964), p. 55.

In order to awake from this sleep and gain consciousness man will have to check his inertia and negativeness. He will have to unite himself once again with nature and understand his inseparable relation to it in order to gain balance and harmony.

Celaya affirms that it is the duty of the artist and poet in society to aid man in acquiring this new state of awareness: «La poesía no es un fin en sí, la poesía es un instrumento entre otros para transformar el mundo.»[2] Due to this zealous desire to transform the world, he directs many poems to other artists and poets in an effort to get them to see the necessity of a united and purposeful action on their part if this goal is to be attained.

The dangerous position in which man finds himself in the twentieth century, with its weapons capable of total destruction, makes the poet keenly aware of the immediate need for world transformation. Not only the artist but every man must be responsible in this transformation, says Celaya:

> Invoco a los amantes, los mártires, los locos
> Invoco a los valientes, los héroes, los obreros,
> los hombres trabajados que duramente aguantan
> y día a día ganan su pan mas piden vino
> Invoco a los dolidos. Invoco a los ardientes.[3]

Poets can no longer be neutral. They cannot write only of beauty and happiness; nor can they concern themselves only with the perfection of meter and rhyme:

> Maldigo la poesía cocebida como un lujo
> cultural por los neutrales
> que, lavándose las manos, se destienden y evaden.
> Maldigo la poesía de quien no toma partido hasta mancharse.[4]

The poet must «provocar nuevos actos.»[5] Poetry is a weapon «cargada de futuro.»[6] Celaya's rejection of traditional verse forms and almost prosaic style of most of his verse demonstrates his attitude toward traditional poets whose primary concern was not *lo necesario*.

---

2 *Ibid.*, Introduction, p. 8.
3 Gabriel Celaya, *Poesía urgente*, p. 12.
4 *Ibid.*, p. 50.
5 *Ibid.*
6 *Ibid.*, p. 31.

Celaya's principal poetic technique used to express his ideas is the symbol. If one had to choose one particular adjective to categorize Celaya's poetry most effectively, it would be symbolist. He uses one word or symbol to illustrate a complex of ideas which he then complicates and individualizes by placing them in varying contexts. Consequently the same symbols are extended throughout his work and gradually take on deeper meaning. In his longer dramatic poems he structures his use of the symbol so that one set of characters in the poem will represent a series of fixed ideas presented in other parts of his work. The characters in the dramatic poem *Dos cantatas* serve as an example. The *Ingeniero* is Prometheus and also a part of conscious man as well as the first (or active force) of the three forces Celaya believes exist in all manifestations of life. *Ezbá* is Pandora, and the pattern of all women as well as the second (or passive) force. *Mono* is Epimetheus, unconscious man and the third (or neutralizing) force. This same type of symbolism and structuring of symbols is found in all his long dramatic poems.

Celaya is also an expert in the creation of tone. By careful use of anaphora, punctuation, syntax and rhythm he is able to communicate exactly the feeling and understanding he desires. The type of techniques he uses contributes to the apprehension of the fullness of experience. Understanding or reception becomes in his hands multi-dimensional, an experience in more of one's receiving area than one: emotional, intellectual, moving, and instinctive. One is reminded of Baudelaire's synesthesia; the means, of course, are individual, however the principle is the same.

Celaya's poetry, though intensely serious and not often happy, has a strong positive quality. He communicates forcefully a surge of hope. Although throughout his work he concerns himself principally with man's lack of consciousness and his solitude, his perpetual and seemingly senseless struggle after happiness and meaningfulness, Celaya is nevertheless convinced that man can conquer through truth and effort. He never once loses his strong sense of man's dignity. Freedom and happiness are his right, although he is not born with them.

Scripta humanistica

Directed by
BRUNO M. DAMIANI
The Catholic University of America
COMPREHENSIVE LIST OF PUBLICATIONS*

18. *Estudios literarios en honor de Gustavo Correa.* Eds. Charles
    Faulhaber, Richard Kinkade, T.A. Perry. Preface by Manuel
    Durán. $25.00
19. George Yost, *Pieracci and Shelly: An Italian Ur-Cenci.* $27.50
20. Zelda Irene Brooks, *The Poetry of Gabriel Celaya.* $26.00
21. *La relación o naufragios de Alvar Núñez Cabeza de Vaca,*
    eds. Martin A. Favata y José B. Fernández. $27.50
22. Pamela S. Brakhage, *The Theology of «La Lozana andalu-
    za.»* $27.50
23. Jorge Checa, *Gracián y la imaginación arquitectónica.* $28.00
24. Gloria Gálvez Lira, *Maria Luisa Bombal: Realidad y Fantasía.* $28.50
25. Susana Hernández Araico, *Ironía y tragedia en Calderón.* $25.00
26. Philip J. Spartano, *Giacomo Zanella: Poet, Essayist, and
    Critic of the «Risorgimento.»* Preface by Roberto Severino. $24.00

Forthcoming

* Carlo Di Maio, *Antifeminism in Selected Works of Enrique
  Jardiel Poncela.* $20.50
* Juan de Mena, *Coplas de los siete pecados mortales: Second
  and Third Continuations.* Ed. Gladys Rivera. $25.50
* Barbara Mujica, *Iberian Pastoral Characters.* Preface by Fre-
  derick A. de Armas. $33.00
* Francisco Delicado, *Portrait of Lozana: The Exuberant An-
  dalusian Woman.* Translation, introduction and notes by
  Bruno M. Damiani. $33.00
* Salvatore Calomino, *From Verse to Prose: The Barlaam and
  Josaphat Legend in Fifteenth-Century Germany.* $28.00
* Darlene Lorenz-González, *A Phonemic Description of the An-
  dalusian Dialect Spoken in Almogía, Málaga — Spain.* $25.00
* Juan de Mena, *Coplas de los siete pecados mortales: Second
  and Third Continuations.* Ed. Gladys Rivera. $25.50
* Maricel Presilla, *The Politics of Death in the «Cantigas de
  Santa María.»* Preface by John E. Keller. Introduction by Nor-
  man F. Cantor. $27.50
* *Studies in Honor of Elias Rivers,* eds. Bruno M. Damiani and
  Ruth El Saffar. $25.00
* Susan Niehoff McCrary, *«'El último godo' and the Dynamics
  of the Urdrama,»* Preface by John E. Keller. $27.50
* Giacomo A. Striuli, *«Alienation and 'Black Humor' in the
  Works of Giuseppe Berto».* $26.50
* Giovanni Boccaccio, *The Decameron.* English Adaptation by
  Carmelo Gariano. $30.00

BOOK ORDERS

* Clothbound. *All book orders,* except library orders, must be prepaid and addressed to **Scripta Humanistica**, 1383 Kersey Lane, Potomac, Maryland 20854.
Manuscripts to be considered for publication should be sent to the same address.